D1554445

Dinghy
Team
Racing

Eric
Twiname

Dinghy
Team
Racing

Adlard Coles Ltd   London

Granada Publishing Limited
First published in Great Britain 1971 by Adlard Coles Ltd
Frogmore St Albans Hertfordshire AL2 2NF and
3 Upper James Street London WIR 4BP

Second impression 1971
Second revised edition 1975

ISBN 0 229 11542 X
Filmset and printed in Great Britain by
BAS Printers Limited, Wallop, Hampshire

BUCKINGHAM PALACE

I very much hope that this new Team Racing Competition will give a lot of enthusiastic clubs and club members many happy hours of sailing. Team racing demands rather a different approach and different techniques so this event may well discover some new talent.

It has the further advantage that teams will be able to travel to other clubs and so experience different conditions and new scenery, if only the clubhouse bar.

The races are the important thing of course, but I daresay there will be much to discuss afterwards and I am sure everyone will enjoy the social side of these encounters.

PHILIP

Preface to the Royal Yachting Association's Team Racing Championship programme of 1969 by His Royal Highness The Duke of Edinburgh

Design and illustrations by Graeme Wilson

Acknowledgements

Many people have helped me to write this book and I would like to thank them. Mick Rhodes and Nigel Redfern made many excellent suggestions and criticisms, and the alternative scoring system which appears on page 137 is the result of a discussion with Mick. Rod Jones also made many useful comments. The background and history were provided by John Henderson, the RYA historian, Stewart Morris and G. Sambrooke Sturgess. Arthur Barron very kindly commented on the rules section. Dr Dave Hardwick of Imperial College Fluid Mechanics Department allowed me to use the equipment on which the flow pictures were taken, and Bill Holden was the photographer. Other pictures were taken by Giles Whittaker, Stuart Black, Yachting World magazine, Wavelength and J. E. Wright. The RYA and the Firefly Association were both extremely helpful. But most of all I have to thank many friends for their suggestions ashore and example afloat.

Eric Twiname London 1971

Introduction

It is only in the last three or four years that team racing has become widely popular in this country but there are few dinghy sailors who have not tried team racing or at least know roughly what it is. Up to now the only way to learn has been to get into a boat and team race, as there has been very little written on the subject. In this book Eric Twiname has put that right at one go, and anyone who knows a little about ordinary racing can pick up the theory of team racing, even though he has still to get on to the water to find out what it is really like.

There is a big difference between ordinary points racing and team racing, and for this reason many people are apt to look at it as a cut-throat type of game where anything goes—this is far from the truth. The fact is that some manoeuvres are used in team racing which no one would ever dream of using in a points race but these manoeuvres are part of the game—an essential part of the game. I suppose there is some sort of comparison with the Rugby schoolboy who picked up the soccer ball and started to run; he broke the rules of soccer but started a new game. While the rules of team racing are basically the same as for points racing, the racing is taken nearer to the limit of the rules but it is definitely not part of the game to take it beyond.

The tactics are more interesting and play a big part in the racing. As well as the extra interest this gives, I find it also very good practice for individual races. The two go hand in hand, and it is hardly surprising that this book contains a lot that is also applicable to individual racing. For the increasing number of newcomers to team racing as well as those who already participate, this book will prove invaluable.

Mike Arnold

Contents

What is Team Racing?

Team races take place between two teams over fairly short courses. Each team has an equal number of boats, usually three but sometimes four, and they are all of the same class. A match normally consists of two races, and to cancel out any differences in boat speeds, teams swap boats between races.

The fundamental difference between team and individual competition is that in team racing, matches can sometimes be won, not by sailing flat out for the finish line, but by deliberately slowing down and delaying someone on the other side. It is this extra tactical interest and also the opportunity for clubs to sail against one another —an opportunity team competition provides and individual does not—which has made team racing as popular in Britain as it is today.

Team racing as we know it started in 1921 with the first of the British-American Cup series sailed in Six Metres, four a side. The series continued intermittently up to 1955. As numbers dwindled in the Six Metre class the International 14's were growing rapidly and in 1933 a series in 14's began between Britain and America, later to include Canada, Bermuda and New Zealand, which continues today. With the rapid spread of one-design dinghies since 1945 team racing has increased in popularity. The spread of team meetings all over the country, mainly in the Firefly class, culminated in 1969 in the first National Team Racing competition which 260 teams entered— a fifth of all sailing clubs in Britain. A spectacular increase since 25 years ago when only a handful of expert helmsmen knew anything about the sport. After the British National competition a European Championship was held for the first time.

In its second year the National Championship attracted an even bigger entry, 352 clubs. The standard of helmsmanship in this competition is exceptionally high as each club enters the best sailors that it can offer.

The scoring system is basically the same as for individual competition: $\frac{3}{4}$ point for first place; 2 for second; 3 for third and so on down to last place. A boat retiring receives 7 points and one disqualified 10, unless the match is being sailed under the alternative penalty system, when a boat which concedes an infringement takes an additional 2 points and one which does not concede and loses the protest, 4 points. The winning team is, of course, the one with the lower score. The scoring is extremely important in the racing, and you will probably appreciate most easily how it works out by taking a close look at the

Winning combinations for White   one race.

Finishing positions	1	2	3	4	5	6	White wins by
1 2 3	○	○	○	●	●	●	$9\frac{1}{4}$
1 2 4	○	○	●	○	●	●	$7\frac{1}{4}$
1 2 5	○	○	●	●	○	●	$5\frac{1}{4}$
1 2 6	○	○	●	●	●	○	$3\frac{1}{4}$
1 3 4	○	●	○	○	●	●	$5\frac{1}{4}$
1 3 5	○	●	○	●	○	●	$3\frac{1}{4}$
1 3 6	○	●	○	●	●	○	$1\frac{1}{4}$
1 4 5	○	●	●	○	○	●	$1\frac{1}{4}$
2 3 4	●	○	○	○	●	●	$2\frac{3}{4}$
2 3 5	●	○	○	●	○	●	$\frac{3}{4}$
1 2 R	○	○	●	●	●	○ rtd	$2\frac{1}{4}$
1 3 R	○	●	○	●	●	○ rtd	$\frac{1}{4}$

diagram above. It shows all the possible winning combinations for White in a single race.

In a close race quick calculation of the score is vital since tactics depend so much on whether you are winning or losing. With a scoring sheet like the one above in the boat, the crew can quickly tell the helmsman how his team stands. A similar table can be made out for four boat teams, but this book deals with the most common form of team racing, three-a-side. The principles are the same however many boats on each side, but with more than four the contest becomes too confusing to enable anyone to make team tactics work.

How can a team race be won by slowing down then? Why not just sail to finish as soon as possible? The answer is best given by looking at a race which a team is losing with positions 2, 4, 5.

The match is to be decided in this instance on one race only and the helmsmen are sailing at an even enough speed to prevent the white boats from improving their positions by speed alone. Now instead of making their boats go faster, which they have already failed to do, White make the opposition go slower; and the opponent that can usefully be slowed is the black boat in third place. White A slows him and the position becomes:

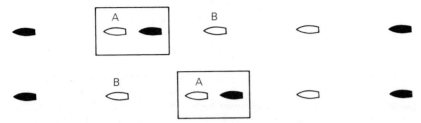

which gives a $\frac{3}{4}$ point lead to White. If White then hold these positions to the finish, they pull off a victory that would have been impossible by simply sailing as fast as possible.

In a race, this sort of slowing manoeuvre most often occurs on the beat, though it is possible on a reach. White boat A covers the black boat astern, keeping her right in the centre of wind shadow so that wherever she goes she sails in dirty wind; this slows her a little and the more she tacks to escape, the slower she goes. Delaying tactics can even work when the two white boats are behind the victim. One white boat challenges the opponent from behind which forces him to defend his position by covering. Once committed to cover, he is to a large degree under the influence of the boat behind: wherever the pursuer goes the covering boat must follow. So now the victim is led away to an unfavourable part of the windward leg, taken on the wrong windshifts or short tacked to a standstill by the attacker, who, in the process allows his teammate to make off at top speed and overtake them both.

Tactics can therefore win a team race sometimes when speed alone can not. On the other hand, a team which sails appreciably faster than their opposition leaves them behind, no matter how good the losers' tactics. These are the two extremes and tactics are normally a compromise between the two, so that a helmsman often has to ask himself 'Do I go for the finish as fast as I can or do I hold back?' And what is more difficult, he has to try and find the right answer.

There is another facet of team race tactics which has an important effect on the racing: a team sails faster en bloc when teammates avoid one another and are prepared to waive the right of way rules among themselves. It would be pointless, for instance, for a starboard tacker to put a teammate about when by bearing away a few feet the starboard man could have taken the avoiding action. At marks, too, there is nothing to be gained by snatching a late overlap on a teammate and forcing him wide. Nor is there any sense in teammates sitting in each other's wind. The best teams work smoothly together and when two teammates meet, the one who would lose least always gives way; finishing order among members of the same side is irrelevant.

The team which looks at a race in this way raises the contest to a duel; the battle is no longer one of six boats whose finishing scores are calculated afterwards to give the winning team. Instead, three boats of one side work together towards the defeat of the opposition. That is the ideal and in close competition with evenly matched teams that is what happens on the water.

When the contest becomes a duel, then a defence/attack situation is produced which has a fundamental effect on the approach to the race. One team wins and the other loses, second is last. The individual race provides a sliding scale of success from first to last, where last may be over a hundredth. Success to an average helmsman short of the top flight may well be, say, fifth if this is higher than his usual position. In the team contest there is no grading of success, the losers lose and the winners win. This means in practice that the race leaders adopt a basically defensive approach and their opposition attack. The underdogs can afford to take an out-and-out attacking line as they have nothing more to lose than what they are already in the process of losing—the race. In close competition it is this battle state which brings a level of tactical interest beyond anything you could find in individual racing.

Each member of the side has to know from one moment to the next whether his team leads or not. Many of his tactical decisions are reversed by a change in the race leadership. Yet there is no score-board on the shore, each man is his own scorer, and he has to know what place changes would switch the lead. When everyone on the team knows exactly what the position is, they can work together to improve it if they are losing or defend it if winning.

Matching teams of fairly similar standard is desirable because in an unequal match there are no tactics. In other sports, however poorly matched the sides, there is nearly always some contact between opposing players. But not in team racing ; a much stronger team leaves the other behind on the first leg and there follows a procession to the finish—which makes the business of pairing up sides of equal calibre an important aspect of good, close racing.

In many ways team tactics resemble a game of chess. If it helps the overall plan a piece may well be sacrificed in chess, just as in team racing you can sometimes help your teammates by sacrificing your own position. The pieces (boats) can make certain moves ; each piece, however brilliantly moved, cannot win without the support of the others. The moves are fairly simple on the water but the time between them is uncomfortably short; and throughout, the tactician has much of his mind and body taken up with handling a potentially un-cooperative boat. Nevertheless, the comparison is helpful and the following principles of chess also apply to team racing strategy :

make a strong opening, think several moves ahead, anticipate opponent's moves and do not crowd your own pieces—there is a lot of sailing in those few chess principles.

The rules of racing are the framework which confine the game to set limits, they dictate what can be done by a boat and what can not. Within the confines of team racing, with its close manoeuvring and quick thinking, a good working knowledge of these rules is essential. No use to decide from the start not to mix it with other boats, to sail a lone course out of everybody's way, that may not be the way the others want it—not if they are losing anyway. Without a working knowledge of the law it becomes very difficult to decide the best course of action at times: to know whether taking the overlap is allowed, whether the nearby boat can be hailed to go about for an obstruction ahead, or the rights and wrongs of a hundred events. The rule book has quite definite views about all these; it is up to the helmsman to be sure that his own views on the situations coincide with the law. Incidents arising from differing interpretations of the rules—or differing stories of what actually happened—are settled by the inevitable protest committee meeting.

Because the main thrill of team racing is a straightforward tactical battle on the water, it is out there in the boat that the rules are of most use. A thorough knowledge tends to limit the number of incidents which go to protest—in itself very desirable, for the racing loses a lot of its point if the result is decided in conclave ashore.

There are a few general principles, then, which apply when you are team racing:

1 sail fast unless there is clearly something to be gained by slowing down an opponent;

2 cover opponents and generally hinder them as much as possible, and at appropriate times make a point of slowing one of them down;

3 always avoid teammates if your own avoiding action is likely to be less wasteful than theirs—no matter who has right of way under the rules;

4 know enough about the rules to be sure of your rights in most situations that arise in the course of racing.

The chapters that follow are based on these four points. Up to page 58 the book covers the more basic and simple sides of the sport, and although this part may be useful to people who have team raced a good deal, it is meant primarily for those who have raced in individual competition, but not in team races. Thereafter the plot thickens and we get into some of the more advanced and complicated tactics of top-level team racing.

The Skills of Beating

Speed in the absence of other boats

The windward leg is always the most tactically involved in a team race. When beating, a helmsman has always a choice between two tacks and in uniformly stable conditions of sea and wind, free from the interference of other boats, the choice of which tack to take at any time would be unimportant: both would provide an equally fast route to the weather mark. But the conditions are never stable or constant. There are always wind or tidal variations at any moment which favour one of the two tacks a helmsman can choose.

If a helmsman can make the most of these natural conditions, his decisions on which tack to take then relate only to wind and water. But the race is not just against the clock, it is against other boats, which, by their closeness also influence the choice of the favoured tack. With individual competition it stops there; a helmsman strives first of all to make the best use of the natural conditions and secondly to limit the adverse effect of nearby boats.

Team racing, as we have already seen, introduces a third factor which has a powerful influence on tactical choice. A helmsman is not just racing for his own position, he has teammates and opponents to consider. The teammates are to be helped as far as possible and the opposition hindered—a dimension is added to individual racing.

For the sake of clarity in talking about the extra complexity which team racing brings, windward work in this book is split into skills and tactics—the techniques and their use. The techniques are those of fast sailing and influencing opponents (covering and slowing, for example); tactics describe when and where to use these techniques. For instance, covering an opponent with wind shadow to slow him is a technique and deciding when to use it is tactics. The distinction is not a rigid one but is valuable in that it highlights the difference of approach essential to team racing.

Although speed is vital, relatively little space is given to it here since this is not primarily a book on how to make a boat go fast, but in a strange boat there are several points particularly to watch for, points of helmsmanship and boat tune.

1 Correct sail trim for the conditions: jib not too hard in a light air or too free in a blow and main set at the most effective angle. Setting up of the sails carefully on the shore is well worth the effort. Halyard, kicking strap and mainsail outhaul tensions have quite an effect on the set of the mainsail and should all be adjusted to give the best sail shape for the wind conditions.

2 The fore-and-aft trim of the hull in the water affects the windward performance and teammates can check each other on this over the water before the start.

3 In strong winds a dinghy sails fastest upright. How this is achieved, whether by pinching or spilling when actually sailing or by flattening sails on the shore before racing, depends on the class, but the need to sail at no more than a few degrees of heel in heavy weather is common to all dinghies.

4 Gusts are a bonus if they are used well and a handicap if their intrusion is an embarrassment; mastering them is well worth the effort. Sailing for the windstrength of the moment, however short the moment, is the key to it. The gust can be picked out on the water before it arrives, and if it brings 10 seconds of force 6 sail for force 6, then when it passes and the wind drops to force 2 (again perhaps only for 10 seconds) sail as in force 2. Helming for average force 4 is too inflexible an approach to make the best of such variable conditions.

5 Waves are a handicap when sailing to windward, but their slowing effect can be minimised by understanding how to ride them and watching the water just ahead in choppy going. The secret is always to keep the bow from driving into an oncoming wave, but at the same time to point as high as possible; this calls for far more helm movement than still water sailing. It is the easy motion of the hull through the water and not the precise angle of a jib or burgee to the wind which becomes almost the obsession of a successful helmsman working to windward in a choppy sea.

With the boat moving well through the water, the fastest windward course depends now on choosing the right moments to tack. (There are no other boats about yet, remember, the race is solely against the natural conditions). The wind direction fluctuates in offshore winds and on inland water, it oscillates like a pendulum about a mean, so that the ideal course to windward is, typically:

(The boat sails at 45° to the wind.)

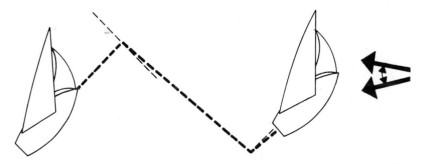

Each tack coincides with a heading shift so the course made good is better than 90° each time and the distance sailed to the weather mark is reduced.

The shifts are not always substantial and spotting them accurately becomes a major occupation of the beat, since to be in phase with them is a great boost and to pick the wrong ones is expensive both in distance and morale. The direction of sailing in relation to the shore, the way the boats ahead point, and the luffing of the jib on a steady course are all pointers to these shifts. The oscillations themselves tend to help too ; a header usually follows a good lift—the pendulum effect. With practice, even small variations can be picked out.

Although these fluctuating shifts are most common, the wind sometimes follows a systematic direction change up the windward leg.

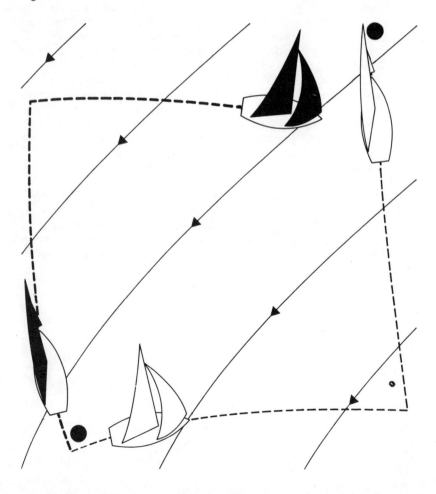

The two alternative course lines sketched into the wind pattern show the direction of two boats travelling equally fast making 45° to the wind. Clearly the best way to sail up a systematic shift is by tacking first towards the inside of the curve. The shift is usually caused by a large natural feature—a valley, a mountain or a bay. When the sailing area is bounded by one of these features the possibility of a systematic shift in the wind direction is easily tested. If a dead run before the start right down the beat gives a curved course, then the wind shifts systematically and in the race the boat should always be sailed towards the inside of the curve.

Apart from this constant curved pattern, the wind may also fluctuate every few seconds in the nature of an offshore wind. The two types of windshift sometimes operate at once: the gradual curve in the wind caused by the geography of the place, and the time dependent, oscillating shifts of the offshore wind disturbing this fixed pattern. The windward leg is then best sailed by making good use of the fluctuating shifts but all the time biasing the tacks towards the course favoured by the systematic shift—that is, the inside of the wind curve.

From wind shifts now to the act of tacking: a wasteful but essential part of the race which, particularly in team races, ought to be done as well as possible. The more confined the water and the more involved the tactics, the greater the need for smooth efficient tacking. River sailors realise this and have evolved a method of roll tacking which in medium weather almost eliminates any distance lost in going about.

1 Helmsman allows the boat to head up.

2 He heels the boat over on top of himself while still sitting in the same place.

3 He crosses the boat and with the main sheeted in brings her upright on the new tack.

The technique requires practice since the degree of roll varies considerably with different wind conditions and from one class of dinghy to another. It even works on the bigger dinghies. Some leading British 505 sailors, for example, perform what is a subdued roll every time they tack in medium and light weather.

Shooting a mark
One manoeuvre which enables you to round a windward mark that you are not quite able to lay without tacking can be extremely useful on the short rounds of a team race course. The procedure is to pinch as high as reasonably possible to lay the mark on the approach, but in the two or three lengths before the mark pick up full windward sailing speed by sailing her full and fast, then, at the last moment, release the jib completely and throw the boat almost head to wind.

The boat's way now carries her to windward and when the mark comes abeam you simply bear off and make the rounding. In medium and light weather this works excellently and it is surprising how far a dinghy will carry her way in these conditions. Apart from the ground you save by avoiding two quick tacks, you have the advantage of retaining your rights over any boats which may be coming up from astern. With just a little daring (the position does sometimes tend to look impossible as you approach the mark, unable to lay it) you can extricate yourself from many a tight situation by shooting a mark.

In the vicinity of other boats

Windshadow
The wind pattern round the rig of a beating boat looks like this:

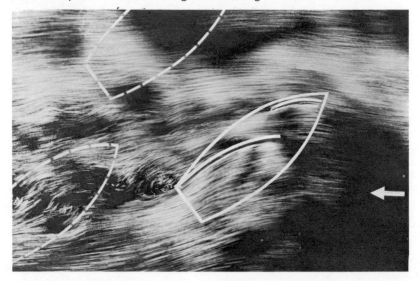

This and all the other flow pattern photographs are taken over a water tank. No valid measurements could be taken from these pictures and applied to sail design, but the picture does give a clear visual picture of flow round sails. Points to notice are:

1 Exact position of a boat suffering most turbulence (extreme left) further aft than popularly supposed.
2 Position of the boat which is not slowed at all by dirty wind.
3 Large deflection in the flow giving a header to a boat on starboard tack and a lift on port.
4 Distance from the sails at which the flow is deflected.
5 Flow begins to bend before it reaches the boat.
6 Speed of flow—where flow lines are closer speed is greater.

The dark and light patches have no relevance to the flow pattern, they result from varying concentrations of the trace powder on the surface.

Close covering In the defence/attack pattern of a team contest defensive covering plays a big part on the windward leg, an opponent following closely must be held off. The surest way of achieving this is to have him sail in dirty wind all the way; and as the outcome of the race may depend on his staying behind, close covering properly done is a match winner.

If a man is challenging on a beat and the decision has been made to cover him, he should be covered relentlessly. The defending boat is positioned so that its wind shadow lies directly over the attacker, and until the end of the leg the following boat sails continually in the other's secondhand air stream.

Every tack the second man makes must be followed by the leader no matter how frequently the tacks come. Wind shifts can be ignored, the object of the exercise is to hold the opponent at a distance.

A duel of this sort obviously highlights tacking skill.

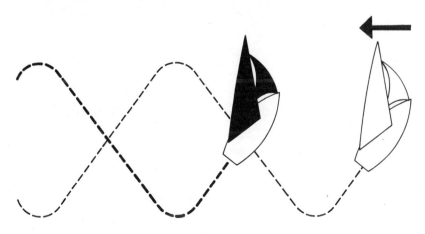

Throughout the book White and Black appear in the diagrams. All the moves are described from the point of view of the White team, and if you think of yourself belonging to White the diagrams are easier to follow.

If tacking happens to be a weakness of White's, Black can break clear by exploiting the weakness in a sharp sequence of tacks. On the other hand, if White makes a few feet at every tack, the pressure is taken off and Black's helmsman is inclined to resign himself to his quota of dirty wind. The man who goes about smoothly and efficiently enters the fray with a very useful advantage. If he also remains calm under pressure he will usually dominate a close tacking match.

480 is covering correctly so that 118 is slowed and headed. If 480 is intent on staying ahead of 118 her helmsman must cover tack for tack; he must watch his opponent closely and sail his own boat with as little attention as he reasonably can. The important thing is to keep 118 right in the middle of his own boat's wind shadow.

Slowing a boat from a lee-bow position
The lee-bow position is tactically a very strong one and used properly forces the windward boat into tacking, as the only alternative is to fall back and to leeward. The key to gaining the initiative from leeward is a tack in the right place.

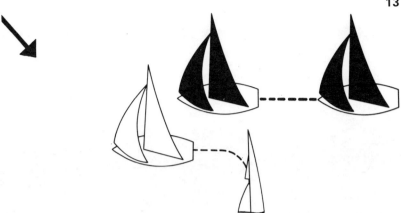

A lot depends on the type of boat and wind speed in judging the moment to tack. The only way to develop skill here is to practise in different conditions and be reasonably (but not too) bold. Having set up the position the weather boat can be killed, stopped almost in her tracks, by continuous and vigorous pinching. Wind shadow does the rest, for as the windward boat bears away to gain speed she falls deeper into dirty wind.

It follows that as soon as the man in the windward boat sees that the lee-bow is a good one he must put about immediately if he can. Better straight away with nothing lost than half a minute later three lengths down.

An immediate tack by Black prevents White following close or she would herself fall into a lee-bowed position.

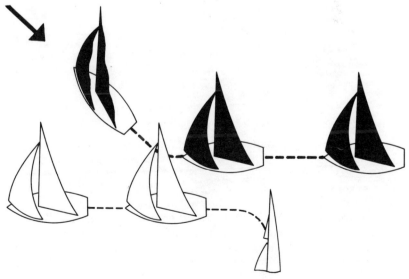

Although White has the initiative by tacking close to lee-bow in the first place, Black loses little ground if she tacks immediately and she sails away with clear wind.

The following pair of pictures was taken during the 1970 RYA National Team Racing final between Felixstowe Ferry and London Corinthian.

The Corinthian boat, second from the left, has just tacked into an excellent lee-bow position under Mike Arnold of Felixstowe, and is pressing home his advantage by heeling the boat a shade to windward

to give maximum dirty wind. If Arnold held on he would be severely slowed, so almost immediately he tacks off gaining clear wind and the opportunity to overtake the Corinthian boat if the windshifts work out well. Notice the pronounced roll as he tacks.

Forcing an opponent to overstand

A boat's progress is neatly impaired if she is made to sail away from the course. A convenient way of arranging this is to force her to overstand the weather mark.

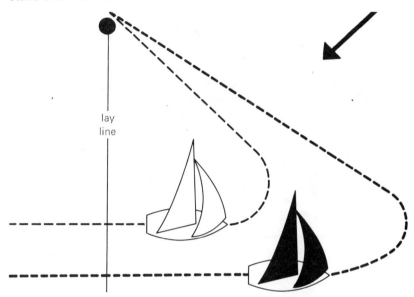

lay
line

White prevents Black from tacking and sails as far past the lay line as necessary to let a teammate through. White is potentially in a vulnerable position, she must pinch if she is not to be lee-bowed too strongly and lose her hold. The danger of Black's lee-bow working is increased if she is to be held on for some distance, but as this is not usually necessary—a few lengths are often enough—the manoeuvre is quite safe.

These are some of the simpler skills of windward work which equip you straightaway to team race, to sail in a way which makes things difficult for the opposition while making as good a contribution to your own side's position as possible. The problem now is how best to use these basic skills in actual race situations : when to sail as fast as possible, when to cover, when not to cover, when to slow someone down on the other side—in fact the whole business of tactics. The next chapter deals with the more basic and straightforward tactics, while chapter 7 goes into some of the refinements which are probably more interesting to someone who has done some team racing, but may perhaps confuse you at first if you are new to the sport.

Beat Tactics

What is a helmsman trying to do in a team race? Firstly, he tries to win by speed—and this goes for his teammates too, so they keep out of each other's way as far as possible; and secondly, he tries to win by preventing opponents immediately astern from overtaking; and thirdly, if his team is not going to win by speed alone, he looks for a chance to slow down someone on the other side and let a teammate past.

There is a lot to think about, but with a little practice and some thought to the ideas that follow here, a team race can quickly be transformed from an individual race for six boats whose points are added together at the end, into a match in which one group of three helmsmen are trying from the start to beat the other three.

Slowing the opposition

Opponents sail more slowly in dirty wind and there, generally, they should stay. By defensive covering, forcing opposition boats to over-stand marks and using the lee-bow position, the race can be made as awkward as possible for the opposition, which after all is an important part of the battle. Yet this same defensive covering and lee-bowing can become a powerful attacking weapon when the situation demands. We can see this by taking a look at the ways in which a team who are in a close losing position can save themselves. How can they break through?

Success depends on attacking the opposition's weak point. In a 1, 3, 6 winning combination for example, the man in third position is particularly vulnerable and if he drops a place the other side take a three quarter lead. This third man is in a much more precarious position than the first man because he has an opponent ahead of him. The leader here is vulnerable, certainly, but only in the same way as any race leader: to be overtaken he must be outsailed by the second man. No outsailing is necessary to bring down number three to fourth place, only a little teamwork.

In the situation that follows, the black boat lying in third place is to be dropped back to fourth. White are losing by a margin of $1\frac{1}{4}$ points and need to gain one position only to take the lead. One place change between two opposing boats makes a difference of 2 points between the teams.

Close covering

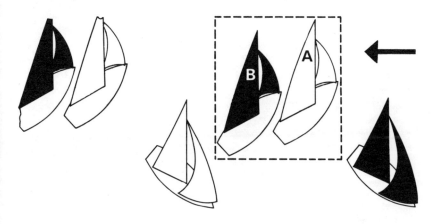

A simply close covers B, tack for tack, B must then accept constant dirty wind and the following white boats gain. If Black wriggles hard by tacking a lot the white boats gain faster. An impossible situation for B if A persists in close covering; one of the white boats behind goes through into third place and White's order becomes 2, 3, 5 giving a threequarter point lead. This combination of 2, 3, 5 is a strong one, the leader can disappear over the horizon for all White are concerned, because further back in the fleet three White boats are very well placed to fight off two opponents. By working together White should be able to let their last man into fourth place and take a two and threequarter point lead. Matches usually consist of two races not one, but the principle is exactly the same in each race.

Passing a boat back behind a teammate is possible not only when one of the teammates is ahead—that is with the opponent sandwiched; surprising as it may seem at first, an opponent can be slowed considerably by a following boat.

When an opponent immediately ahead close covers you, you automatically dictate his tactics. Wherever you go about he goes; if you tack often, he tacks with you. In all but the lightest winds tacking is wasteful, so by making your opponent tack frequently in his efforts to cover you, you slow him down. If you then engage your opposite number in a tacking battle, leaving a teammate astern to sail his beat unhindered in clear wind, the chances are he will overtake both the opponent ahead and yourself. Once ahead, your teammate can closely cover the opponent and allow you to overtake. By working together in this way, two boats can overtake an adversary who sails at an identical speed.

A good team racing helmsman will always be looking at his team's position to find this sort of opening. After all he may be the one who is in a position from which he can slow an opponent and win the match. When you are losing you should always ask yourself 'Can I slow down the opponent astern, and if I do is there anything to be gained?' Mostly there will be nothing you can do by slowing, but sometimes, as in the example above, the manoeuvre is a match-winner. Tempting as it may be to chase the opponent ahead, the match can more easily be won by delaying the man behind.

Slowing a boat by luffing
Luffing an opponent on the windward leg to hold him up only works when either he cannot tack or will sail further if he does.

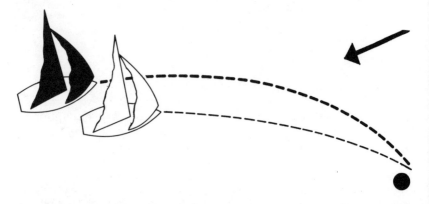

Although Black is being slowed severely by White, Black's skipper does better to hold on than to tack and sail further.

Breaking out of cover in a duel
There are a variety of ways, then, in which an opponent's boat may be slowed to advantage on the windward leg, either from ahead or by a boat close astern. But circumstances may not favour the slowing of an opponent; instead the result may hinge on a straight duel, boat for boat. There are several ways in which a boat may break clear of another's cover and overtake her, or at least get close enough to attack on the next downwind leg.

By tacking on the heading shifts and moving fast through the water it is possible to close on the boat ahead—even when she is covering attentively. At about three length's distance you can get no closer by using the shifts, for at this range the wind shadow of the covering boat becomes too powerful. Now the problem is to throw off this wind shadow. It can often be done by tacking in the right places.

The tack here by White gives A the dilemma of tacking close in her team-mate's wind or leaving White. If A sails on, White is still in dirty wind but not so seriously as before and, if the port tack is favourable, will gain on A when they meet again.

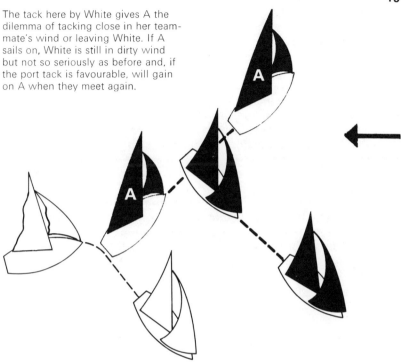

Moored boats can be very useful too. White tacks and Black cannot.

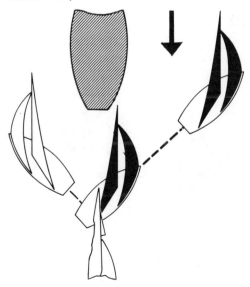

White goes off on her own. Other obstructions—shoals or an island —serve the same purpose. The confidence of Black's helmsman often goes for a time when White makes so good a move. Most courses are not so obliging as to provide moored boats for the benefit of the losing side, but there are other ways of breaking through from behind.

Waves make tacking difficult. The challenger picks the right moments to go about in the oncoming waves, tacks often and concentrates on sailing fast and going about as efficiently as possible. The covering helmsman has his attention split between the threat from behind and his own good tacking. He has only to make one mistake on a wave, a bad tack, and the man behind is away in clear wind with a chance of breaking through.

Without waves a bad tack can often be coaxed from the leader if the pursuing boat makes two or three tacks in very quick succession. Again the threat from behind is likely to divert his attention and force an error if he is made to move fast enough.

Dummy tacks can be very effective but are difficult to do properly. The idea is to make the covering boat's helmsman think a normal tack is being made, then when he is committed you go back to your original tack.

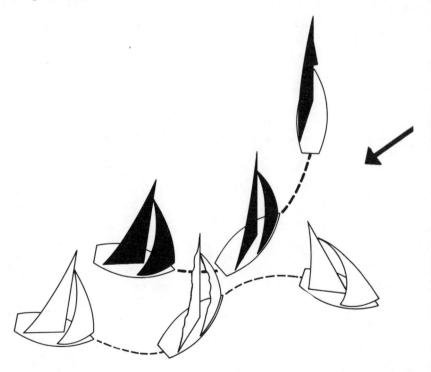

White thus gains clear wind and a great psychological victory over the black boat. Success in selling a dummy depends on lulling the covering helmsman into a tack routine and breaking it unexpectedly —he mustn't expect to be fooled. Deception is easier with a slowish roll tack than with a sharper more violent one because the covering helmsman has to watch for a longer time during the slower tack. The important point is that the dummy should look identical to all the previous tacks right up to the point where it becomes a dummy, the point where the helmsman drops the boat away from head to wind back to the original tack. A loud call of 'Ready about' is suspicious if it didn't precede the earlier tacks. Also, the man throwing the dummy should expect it to fail. If he does, putting the boat head to wind for a length or so loses very little: putting it past head to wind and coming back to the first tack is very wasteful.

Useful as they are in a tight corner, dummies should be used sparingly; their success depends upon surprise.

Defending a lead
So much for the attack, but once a points lead is gained—whether off the start or in the course of the race—it must be defended, and as we saw earlier in considering methods of attack, a slender lead is not always easy to hold—not by defence alone anyway. A 1, 3, 5 lead is held by rigid covering in pairs.

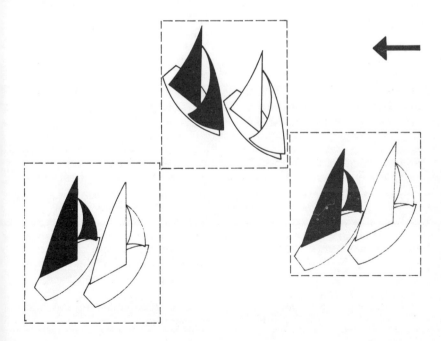

Each white boat close covers and continues to do so right up the beat. Black have a real problem breaking the hold. They can only do it by escaping White's covering tactics or by overtaking on the downwind legs. But in this position:

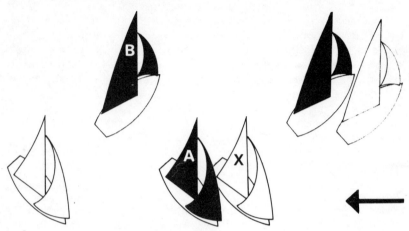

where White X has no teammates to call on and two black boats challenge astern, rigid covering will not enable White to hold the lead. Rigid covering by X would be used by A to force a tacking battle. So how does White's helmsman hold his position?

He switches to loose covering and goes as fast as he knows how, sailing within the approximate triangle formed by the spread of the fleet behind and the windward mark. His chances of holding off the pursuers depend on helming skill alone; he picks the best tacks and makes the best speed through the water. By confining himself to this triangle White's helmsman is unlikely to let both black boats through, and should A pass he is within range to begin close covering B. Until the circumstances change (one pursuer falls back or a place is lost) the White boat X is isolated from her team and has to sail an individual race.

These two examples are clearcut: in the first White must cover religiously, in the second fast individual sailing with only loose cover is called for. Sometimes the involvement of a race makes it difficult to decide what course of action to take but whatever decision you make, stick to it. Almost always the right answer is close covering. A helmsman who picks out one of his pursuers and covers him closely can rarely be criticised, but a man who goes off on his own, letting both past, breaks every tactical principle in the book. So loose covering should be reserved for:

1 The first beat before positions have become clear. Rigid covering takes over when the fleet sorts itself out.

2 A shifting wind with two opponents close behind, and then only when the race would be lost with a place dropped. If one of the pursuing boats drops back then the other should be close covered.

3 The last beat when two opponents are close behind and one place will decide the match.

Dropping an opponent back can be a good move for the leading team, the lead becomes greater and easier to hold. This ploy was once used in a devastating way by West Kirby Sailing Club in the Wilson Trophy competition:

West Kirby white

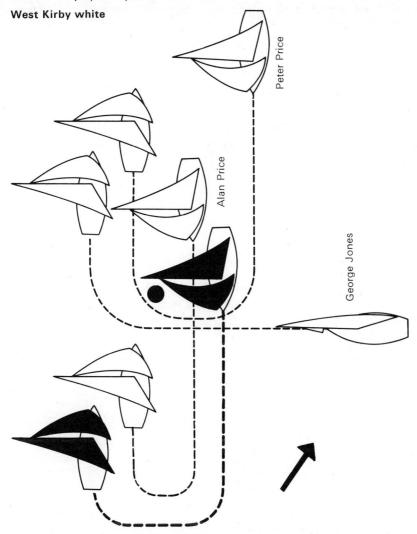

The black boat is the race leader until Alan Price of West Kirby gets on his tail. Twenty seconds later the black boat has been forced to sail past the mark and the whole West Kirby team is through : three places gained in one neat, simple move. A powerful move, and one which can be used, though not always as spectacularly as this, by the leading side in the course of many team races; it is a way of strengthening a leading position by attack.

Anticipation In many of the tactical sequences dealt with so far quick action is called for, and failure to make the right move can be due as much to lack of anticipation as lack of knowledge. You can easily lose a straightforward tacking match with another boat which, by thinking a move ahead you could have won with a tack at the right moment. A typical and quite common instance arises when two boats are on opposite tacks approaching the finish line.

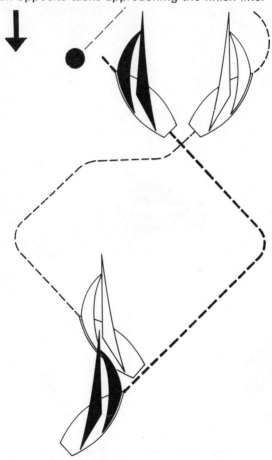

The white boat crosses just ahead of Black, who has a slight edge of speed, and sails on to come into the mark on port tack. Black's starboard approach forces White to bear away round Black's stern and finish behind.

The helmsman of the white boat would have foreseen this turn of events had he thought for a moment about the likely position on the approach to the mark. Persisting with the starboard tack is unlikely to succeed, so he his left with two possibilities: to tack lee-bow under Black on the port tack or to tack immediately upwind.

The lee-bow tack is useless, it ensures that Black can make her tack onto starboard and finish ahead. But a tack close upwind works

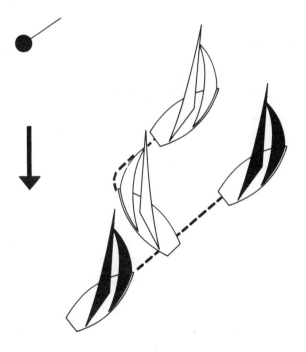

because Black is too close to White to be able to tack for the finish line, leaving White free to tack when she pleases and cross the finish ahead. There is a serious drawback here, though, because Black may choose to tack onto starboard at the same moment as White goes onto port and in a collision during a simultaneous tacking incident the white boat would be out. So the safest move by White is to sail on for two or three lengths, tack onto port upwind and behind. After a few lengths, when Black tacks onto starboard to lay the finish line, White will be able to tack close under her lee-bow and finish ahead.

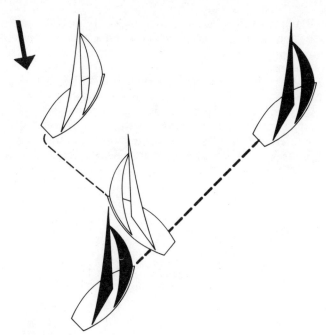

It is certainly easier now to look at the problem and work out the best moment for White's tack than in the excitement of a tense finish. But if White's helmsman gives the matter a little thought when he sees the situation coming, looks just a few lengths ahead, he stands a good chance of making his tack at the right moment—a better chance, anyway, than by leaving it until his opponent's bows loom up beneath the jib.

Keeping clear of teammates and their wind Anticipation is also needed to sail as fast as possible without placing teammates in dirty wind. A teammate is sometimes faced with a situation in which he has little freedom of choice about what to do.

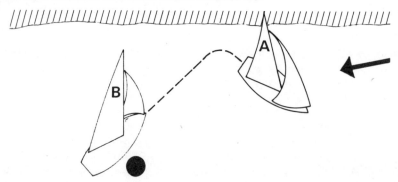

Boat A has not anticipated the likely course of teammate B, with the result that B must either tack into the dirty wind of A or sail in towards the shore and follow exactly in A's wake. Had the helmsman of the leading boat been considering the problem facing his mate at the mark he would have tacked immediately leaving B a clear wind and choice of tacks.

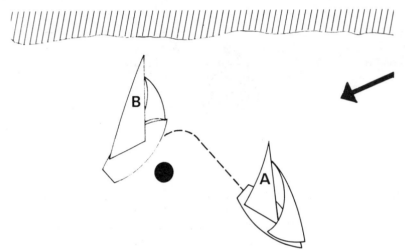

If B then sails on towards the shore before tacking, an opponent following has the problem of her dirty wind.

Although this example is peculiar to confined waters, crossing tacks in open water leads to a variety of situations in which similar anticipation of a teammate's action leaves him clear wind. This happens at its simplest in a good lee-bow.

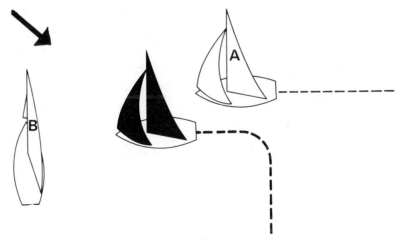

A has just been caught in a good lee-bow position, so close that she should tack immediately to clear her wind. Teammate B is crossing and, if she holds her course, will sit squarely on the wind of A when A tacks away. To avoid this B must look one move ahead and tack:

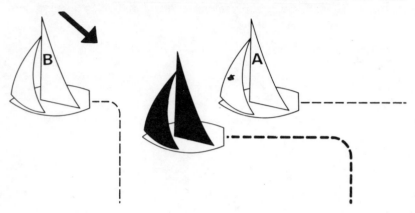

Now A can make her move unhindered and B has an opponent in her wind shadow. On her next tack A should have no difficulty crossing ahead of the black boat which is now sailing in dirty wind.

Had B failed to look a move ahead, her teammate would have faced a strong lee-bow or, if she tacked, dirty wind. By their leader's tack the two white boats have dealt very nicely with the black one.

Waiving rights-of-way Helmsmen of the same team can often help each other if the right-of-way man waives his rights. Port and starboard, tacking in water and claiming water at marks are rights that are often worth conceding to a teammate. The rules allow waiving so long as an opponent is not baulked by the avoiding action of the right-of-way yacht and so long as teammates do not collide.

For instance, the boat which is likely to lose least in avoiding action between team members should give way regardless of rights.

Starboard boat bears away to avoid port tack teammate.

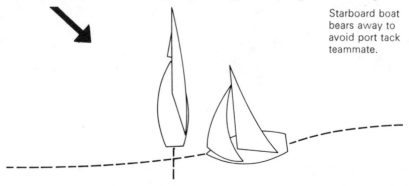

Obviously the starboard tacker here would have caused the port tacker a lot of trouble by insisting on her rights. Less obviously:

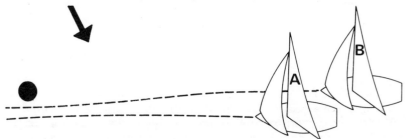

B is making a mistake by taking the overlap and forcing A wide. The answer here is for B to slow and let A off the hook, both then round close to the mark in line with A leading. Less is lost by the following boat slowing than if the leader is pushed wide.

A practised team will waive rights many times in the course of a race without incident or misunderstanding. The secret lies in anticipation, clear, short calls and keeping a good lookout when carrying the right-of-way. A call which goes, 'Bill, there's no need for you to tack, I'll cross behind you' is likely to be received across the water in Force 4 as, 'Bill...tack', not exactly the intended message. Whereas, 'Bill, carry on' is open to very few misinterpretations. So calls must always be short, loud and impossible to misinterpret. 'You tack' or 'I'll tack' is bad because the only word likely to be heard in a crisis is 'tack'—so he does. Far better to fix the calling with the hailed helmsman's name and, perhaps, 'I'm crossing' or 'Carry on' as command calls. 'Starboard' called to a teammate is best used when the opposition are close enough to prevent waiving of rights.

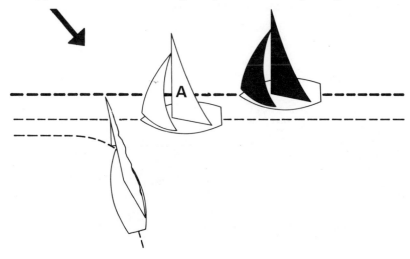

A 'Starboard' call from A leaves his teammate in no doubt (even if he has not already seen Black) that the right-of-way rules apply. Teammates who consistently put each other about for any reason other than opposition influence are not sailing as a team. They tie themselves, rather than their opponents, in knots.

Captaincy It is a lot to expect anyone new to team racing to do the right things to start with, and this is where an experienced team captain can be a big help. There is no harm in the captain telling a less experienced member of a team when to cover someone, which tack to take, or even occasionally when to tack. Admittedly the team's tactics are going to hold no surprises for the opposition if the captain broadcasts his intentions by calling to the rest of the team first, but if the leader knows his stuff the team are likely to work better as a result.

Even in the most expert teams the captain has an important part to play, though his communication then is much more likely to be policy rather than detail. An experienced helmsman will know exactly when to tack to cover for example, but unless specifically asked to do so, may not feel it his job to chase an adversary who has taken an unlikely looking tack away out to one side of the beat. The captain may also prevent people making mistakes. It is often easier to see the best way to handle a situation when viewing from a distance, and a good leader will make a practical suggestion to one of his team who is either doing the wrong thing or is missing an opportunity to slow someone down and gain a place for the side.

After a race, too, the captain is the best man to comment on the way the race was sailed. A word of congratulation to a teammate who sailed well, or a minute or two talking with another about where he slipped up can help considerably in making a team out of three individuals.

Tactics really do work

A fair repertoire of team race skills and tactics has emerged up to this point and this is as far as we need take it at the moment. An experienced team using the various techniques described and using them in the right places can make things very hot for their adversaries.

This point was made perfectly in a race in the quarter-finals of the Wilson Trophy between London University and the Oxford and Cambridge Sailing Society. The helmsmen of both teams are expert in individual racing and also know how to team race. London lead after the first race by one and a quarter points, and the course for the second is:

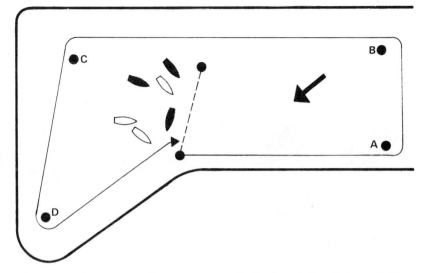

The start of the second race goes to Oxford and Cambridge Sailing Society in a big way so that they lie 1, 2, 3 at the weather mark (A) with London fairly close behind but obviously in dire trouble. This order holds for the downwind legs and at the beginning of the second lap the order at (D) is:

J Vines   G Taylor   S Vines

Stevie Vines is close enough to the third Society boat to draw him into close covering on the windward leg. He is slowed by the engagement, Graham Taylor overtakes and close covers, dropping the Society man behind both his teammates into last place. Now the position immediately after the weather mark is:

G Taylor   J Vines   S Vines

London are looking for one place to gain a tie or two places for a win. Their attention centres on the vulnerable boat of the opposition —number 2. Stevie Vines closes a little downwind and forces the man into a series of wasteful gybes to protect his wind as he approaches mark (C). As a result Jeremy Vines closes.

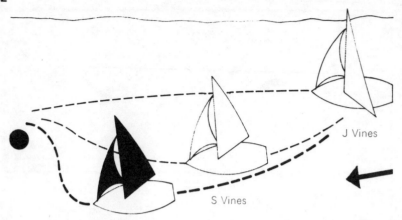

With Stevie Vines now only three lengths astern at mark (D) the Society boat tacks to go for the finish line and Stevie Vines stands on a little before tacking.

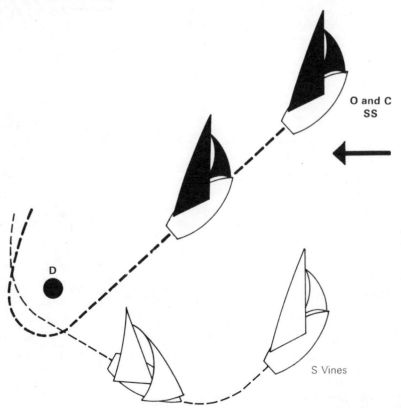

The Society helmsman sees he cannot lay the closest end of the line and decides to protect himself against Stevie Vines upwind.

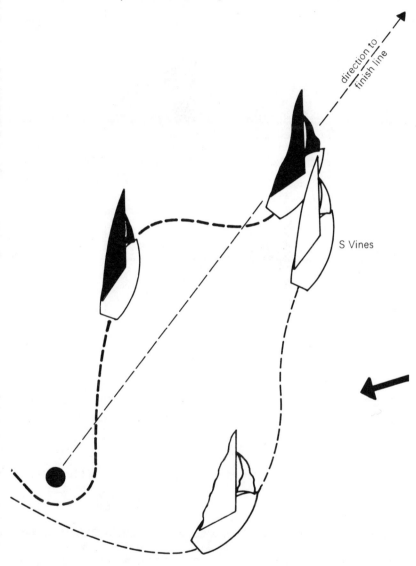

These two tacks have lost him the lead he had and he must content himself with lee-bowing the London boat. A resail now looks likely as Vines should cross ahead of the Society boat when he tacks for the starboard end. But this is what happens next:

34

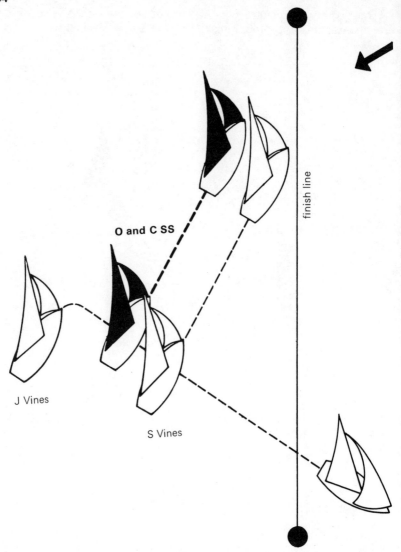

O and C SS

finish line

J Vines

S Vines

Stevie Vines does not tack, he holds on the Society boat to the distant end of the line leaving his brother clear to put in a port tack and cross the line in second place. Stevie then finishes third and the race is won.

So from what appeared a hopeless position against strong opposition the London helmsmen used basic team tactics to climb from that 4, 5, 6 to 2, 3, 5. Working as individuals they would have been well beaten, but as a team they won.

Downwind Part I

The Reach

Boat speed is vitally important on a reach. Tactics play less part than in windward work, but there are still a number of useful manoeuvres that can be used and some mistakes in positioning that ought to be avoided.

Place changes on a reach are usually brought about among team-mates by luffing an opposing boat.

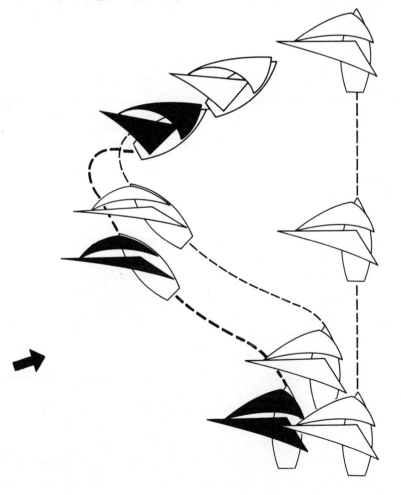

The leading white boat allows a teammate past by luffing Black away off course.

Slowing by blanketing has the same result if the opponent attempts to pass to leeward.

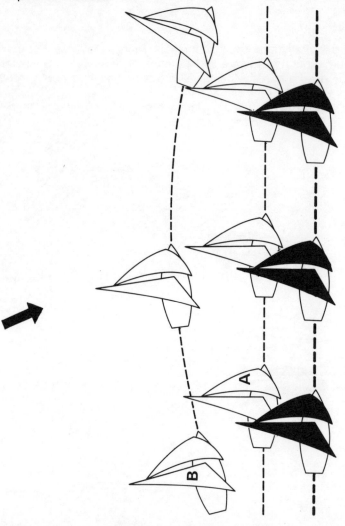

Success here depends on the helmsman of the white boat A slowing himself to allow teammate B past while holding Black in his wind shadow.

In both these operations the boat which is allowed through, the second white boat, should ignore the nearby involvement and sail the best course to the next mark.

Speed on a reach

Boat speed must be a helmsman's main concern whatever is happening nearby. When the boat is not his own, the skipper has to pay even more attention than usual to those factors which make a boat go on the reach. The handling will be a little unfamiliar as each boat, even of the same class, behaves differently in some way. To make it less unfamiliar, reaching up and down to get the feel before the start is a good idea. The points which need particular attention in the race itself are :

1 Trim of the sails is important—always on the point of lifting without actually doing so.

2 Steer a small dinghy as much by angle of heel and sail trim as by use of the helm. The aim is to sail near upright with neutral helm. A slight windward heel helps here. The underwater hull shape of a dinghy heeled a little to windward has a steering tendency equivalent to bearing away with the helm; weather helm is also reduced in a windward heel because the centre of effort of the rig is brought further to windward, which reduces the tendency to screw up into the wind. A further benefit comes in gusty conditions, for a slight windward heel gives the helmsman and crew a better chance of catching planes quickly than when the boat is already heeled to leeward.

3 Concentrate on using waves to the best advantage. Aim to sail downhill all the time ; it is surprising what a difference this can make in a stiff breeze.

4 Good use of a tidal stream is particularly important when the race is against it. Working eddies near a shore and sailing really close in to the shore is the key to success.

5 The wake of the boat ahead can be useful in a blow. The quarter wave is a sort of aquatic tow rope and planing diagonally down it ensures a fast ride, and often the final bonus of a leeward overlap.

6 Watch for gusts, sail upwind before they arrive and bear away in them. This is essential to gain those few extra lengths in variable winds. When the gusts are really powerful the boat can become well nigh uncontrollable as they strike and only become manageable again after hard sitting out and a few seconds' struggle by helmsman and crew. This need not be so. If the gust is seen approaching—and gusts nearly always can be, provided the helmsman looks at the water upwind—the boat can be heeled a fraction to windward before it arrives. As the full force is felt helmsman and crew should already both be sitting out; the initial blow is eased by a quick release of the mainsail to spill wind followed by a flick of the helm to bear away; recovery of complete control is gained by pulling in the mainsheet again and the boat reaches away upright on a

scintillating plane. If the helmsman sees the gust coming a dinghy need not heel, it is when he is taken by surprise that the boat becomes unmanageable.

7 Sail a straight line between marks in a cross tide. Aiming at the mark means sailing further. The most accurate way of sailing the straight line course is to take a transit through the mark to the shore and stick to the line the transit establishes.

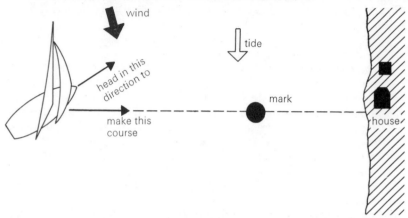

Here the mark lines up with a point just to the right of the two houses. Sailing along this line is simple, no matter how the boat must be pointed to remain on it. So often a fleet performs a semi-circle because the helmsmen cannot judge a straight line between marks, particularly in light airs and strong tides. If the transit shoots out to sea and there is no convenient landmark to fix on, the cloud formation (if it is distinctive) or a distant ship can also be used. Even when clouds or ships move slowly along the horizon, the course sailed on their transit is normally better than the curved course sailed by aiming directly at the mark.

Keeping clear of teammates wind on a reach

Teammates sail fastest collectively when they make the best of the available wind power; on a reach this means spreading out. There is a general rule to follow in deciding whether to sail upwind or downwind of a teammate ahead.

Broad reaching—the following boat goes to leeward
Close reaching—the following boat goes to windward

Teammates stay clear of each other's wind shadow by following this as the diagrams opposite show.

Broad reach When the second boat goes to leeward, she neither slows the leader with her wind shadow nor falls into dirty wind herself. The leading boat can help by working a little to windward.

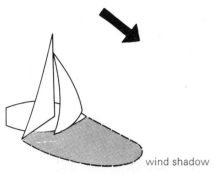 

wind shadow   wind shadow

A broad reach gives an attacker the opportunity to take a wide courses well away from the direct line; and in light and variable conditions that can pay off. However big the attacker's deviation from the straight line course, one defender should sail a similar course nearby to prevent the wanderer from helping himself to any lucky winds.

Close reach When the second boat here goes to windward she does not slow the leader unless she overtakes, nor is she in dirty wind at any time. The leading boat here falls a little to leeward to put more distance between the two boats as the following boat climbs to windward. Agreement about position is made by calling as the leg starts, 'I am sailing the leeward course,' or something of the sort.

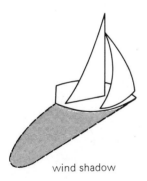 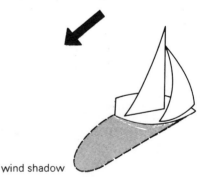

wind shadow   wind shadow

Rounding marks after a reach
Bad mark rounding costs a lot of ground in the short, mark-studded course of a team race. As a general rule round on the inside, even if it means slowing to do so, because the commanding berth for the following leg is the inside one (except perhaps when rounding onto a run).

The purpose of a good rounding is to come out of it as well placed as possible. Thus the second rounding here is much better than the

1 bad rounding   **2** good rounding

first. The initial sacrifice of half a length is entirely justified.

Important as it is to leave marks close, the extra inch is not worth the risk of touching and having to re-round. Among waves on the sea or in a tide a small safety margin is necessary for the rounding. While six inches may be a safe distance to miss a mark by on a lake, a boat's length can be too close in a rough sea with a strong tide flowing. Only practice tells. The important point is that mark rounding is a part of the race and benefits, just as sail trim and windward technique do, from a little thought. When racing at close quarters in a keen contest everything counts, the few feet that become a boat length which becomes a place are always to be found if they are sought hard enough.

The Run

A slender lead is very difficult to hold on the run; a following boat within three or four lengths has a powerful weapon to use, its wind shadow. The photograph that follows gives a very vivid picture of how a running rig affects the air flow. This picture, like the earlier one of a rig close hauled, was taken over flowing water. The 'sails' are vertical metal plates bent to the shape of sails. The surface trace powder is aluminium dust.

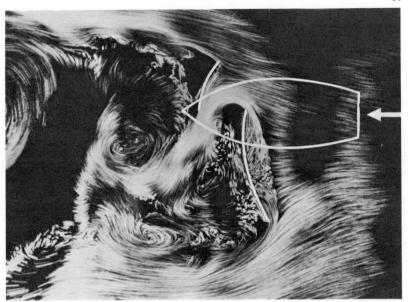

Properly placed, this wind shadow works excellently and is just as effective in heavy weather as in light air because the apparent wind speed is reduced by the forward speed of the boat. Also, planing speeds vary noticeably with small changes in the driving force, so that a well placed wind shadow which reduces this driving force slows down the boat ahead.

The helmsman of the leading boat can do little other than watch the burgee of the boat on his tail and avoid being in its direct line—the burgee's direction roughly marks the centre of the wind shadow. A few gybes when the wind is dead astern make the sail plan a more difficult moving target and help to shake off the blanketing effect.

The best defence on a run is to sail as fast as possible in clear wind. For a leading team this means that the boats spread to clear each other. Spreading is also a safeguard against opposition boats trying to come through by sailing wide of the straightline course. When a helmsman finds his boat sandwiched between two opponents his best course is to remain exactly between them both, this virtually ensures that he beats one of them at the end of the leg.

Places are most surely gained on the run at the leeward mark. An inside overlap snatched here is a certain place gained and unless an outside course has been deliberately chosen to clear a bunch of boats ahead or to cover someone, the leg should be sailed to this end. The rounding at the end of the run is the most difficult one to do well, particularly if it incorporates a gybe. The course change is often about 120° and a good position after the mark is always the goal.

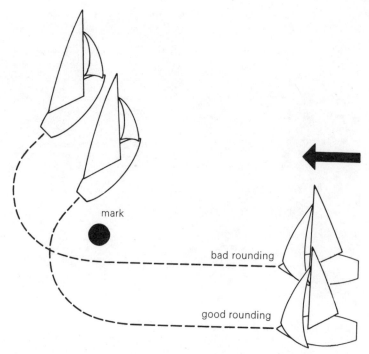

mark

bad rounding

good rounding

In keen competition with boats nearby the manoeuvre becomes even more difficult to do well: yards of mainsheet to pull in, a good approach to maintain while gybing and other boats to watch. Better to practise at leisure and handle the rounding well and confidently than to lose out in a race when it really matters. One of the commonest errors is to sweat the jib in hard too soon before the boat is properly on a close hauled course; this holds the head off the wind, heels her and results in a wide rounding. Jib and main are best hardened together so that the beat begins with the impetus of a reach before the mark—even if this impetus lasts only for a length or two. The boat has to be kept upright on the rounding and this means getting crew weight over the side early, well before the rounding is completed. A dinghy is easily held upright by sitting out early but is much more difficult to bring back to the vertical once heeled.

Starting Part 1

A team starts well when two of its members make good clear-wind starts with the third ahead of at least one opponent. The three helmsmen should be reasonably spread down the line and, to begin with anyway, aim for a crack start. Each should concentrate far more on a good individual start than on worrying about opponents.

Having said that, there are two sides to team starting: firstly, the fastest clear start to get away from the line well placed, and secondly a start which puts the opposition into a bad position by forcing them to start badly or hindering them with wind shadow. The opposition can be luffed over the line, held away from the line and disrupted in various other ways; but the prime object is good individual starting. Once this is fairly regularly achieved some team racing can be introduced. So to begin with how can good starting become routine?

Windward Starts

Boat Control
Control of the boat is essential before the start. The area is congested even with only six boats, so that accelerating and decelerating are as important as direction control. There are three ways of killing a boat's way:

1 Luff head to wind.
2 Let mainsail and jib right out.
3 Back the jib.

A boat can only be stopped naturally when sailing between 45° and 90° to the wind.

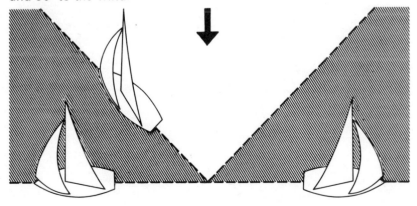

Luffing head to wind is very effective, but on closing with a start line a violent luff is likely to ruin the approach.

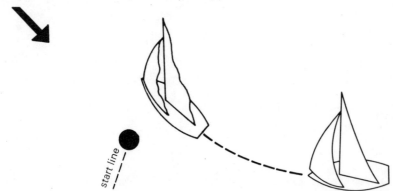

start line

Letting both sails flap in good time would have worked better here. This method needs no alteration of course, but the boat carries its way so there is no strong braking effect. It is, however, easy to do and used soon enough slows the boat in a way that can be regulated by sail trim. The mainsheet becomes almost a hand throttle.

Had the boat above been too late in letting everything go she could have stopped very quickly by backing the jib. The boat stops dead. This can be a very good way of avoiding boats ahead or correcting a miscalculated approach. A word of warning though: unless the crew is briefed beforehand he will probably not believe what is required nor do it promptly. Leeward boats are a constant threat and should be watched, because a stationary boat can be luffed with little chance of responding.

It is easier to accelerate than to slow down in a sailing boat, and for this reason an approach at about half maximum boat speed gives most control. Speed can then be varied at will without losing steerage way.

Tacking before the start, particularly at low speeds from a reach to a reach through 180°, often causes problems but it need not, even in really heavy weather. The technique is to spin the boat with the mainsail. It works when the boat is stopped or moving only slowly but is hazardous at speed.

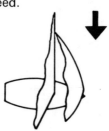

The jib is freed completely before attempting to tack, the main is slack and only partially drawing. The strong pull of the mainsheet is now used to spin the boat round. The technique is simply to forget the helm, let it go, stand up and pull in the mainsheet energetically.

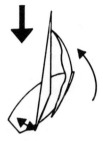

The boat pivots about its centreboard and the angular momentum carries it round onto the new tack. Little effort is required, even when moving slowly in extreme wind conditions. The jib must not be pulled in at any time during the tack or the excessive turning moment needed to spin her is lost when it fills.

Choosing the right end
Unless the start line is perfectly set at right angles to the wind there is an advantage in starting at one end. The better end is the one from which a boat would cross ahead of another which started simultaneously from the opposite end. The line is rarely perfect, so to make a good start a helmsman needs to know which is the favoured end; there are several ways to find this out but the two given below are the best.

A boat with shrouds will sail slowly at right angles to the wind with jib flapping and mainsail right out, and sailing in this leisurely way along the line the wind direction can be found. By sailing on the other tack in the same fashion the accuracy of the test is checked— if she sails at right angles to the wind she returns in exactly the reverse direction. The angle her wake makes with the starting line gives the angle of the bias in the line.

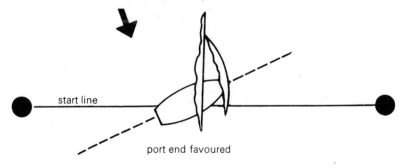

start line

port end favoured

Alternatively, if the boat is to sail in an exact line between the starting marks in each direction with jib and mainsail free she sails faster away from one end.

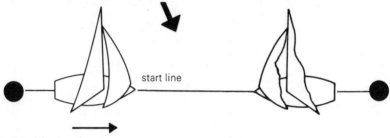

port end favoured

The wind favours the end from which she sails away faster. The advantage of finding out wind direction in this way is that in sailing slowly down the line to start, any shift is quickly picked up—the boat speeds up or slows down according to the direction of the wind change. The decision of which end to start can be reversed if necessary very shortly before the gun.

The most usual way of testing the wind direction on the start line is to throw the boat exactly head to wind and check the direction she points in relation to the line. This is a simple and quick operation, but it does have the big disadvantage in anything of a shifting wind that the direction is known only at the moment before the gun when the test is made, and in the final minutes the direction may swing undetected to favour the other end.

The end favoured by the wind on the line may·not necessarily be

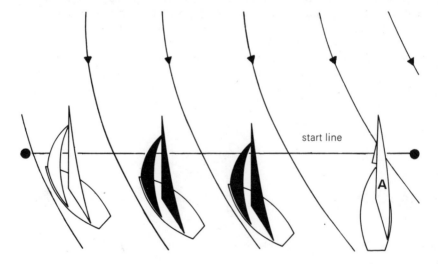

the best place to start. Natural conditions—tide, or systematic windshift, for example—may favour a particular direction on the windward leg. If this is so, the best start is the one which allows the boat to go for this favoured course off the line. For instance the port end in the lower diagram opposite looks like the place to start. But a systematic shift runs the length of the first beat giving an advantage to a long port tack away from the start. The white port tacker A, starting at the apparently unfavourable end, is sure of clearing away from the line on the desired tack, sacrificing the immediate advantage of the port end to be able to do so.

The reasons for favouring this start may be tide advantage to starboard, stronger wind to starboard, smoother water to starboard or a systematic wind shift.

Judging the approach
When the starting policy has been decided the skipper must go for the selected point of the line on the gun with full speed and clear wind. As this is the part which causes most trouble we can look at it in two progressive steps, first of all without any other boats about and then with. The first, perhaps, seems an artificial way of looking at starts because there are always boats milling around and it is these that often seem to throw a helmsman in his approach. But is it the other boats solely? Is it not that very often the starting plan is rather vague before other boats come anywhere near? If a starting plan is made and practised before the five minute gun it becomes a pattern by which to start. You then know exactly how you are going to get to the chosen point as the gun goes. Once you have rehearsed your set piece with no other boats about, your aim on the real start is to prevent nearby boats from disrupting your approach.

First then, a few minutes before the start you make a timed approach, counting down as though it were the real thing. The angle of approach is important: a reach parallel to the line is vulnerable if too broad for it invites a luff, a close hauled course leaves no latitude for avoiding boats, becomes difficult to control and gives a lot of leeway at low speeds. A close reach usually works best. If the first dress rehearsal is a failure—too soon, too late, unable to lay the line—a repeat or two irons out major misjudgements. The approach can be fast or slow, but up to 10 seconds to go a slowish approach gives more control than a fast one as accelerating is easier than stopping—boats are not designed with brakes (though it is interesting that Manfred Curry, the father of racing tactics, raced a scow on Lake Geneva with brakes in the nineteen twenties before the rules forbade them). Yet however the true start is to be made it should follow the pattern of the practised ones. You should now be able to make a well-judged practice start without other boats about, and by now should have a fairly accurate idea of the time it takes to cover distance in the conditions prevailing.

An allowance of a few seconds has to be made over the practice start when it comes to the real one, a little time in hand is needed for avoiding other boats. Steering clear of a boat ahead on the same tack can only be done in two ways, either to port or starboard, which means that as a straightforward obstruction she presents little problem. Deciding which side to go, though, is made more difficult by the wind shadow to leeward and the possibility of a luff in overtaking to windward.

The lee-bowed position on a start line is a killer and has to be avoided. So if there are a few seconds in hand on the approach the leeward side of the boat ahead is probably best as:

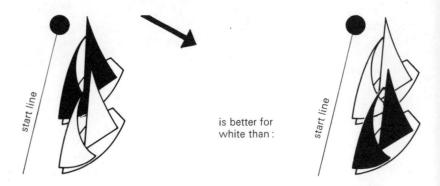

is better for white than:

If she decides to overtake to windward White may be able to avoid the lee-bow. She must climb well away from Black,

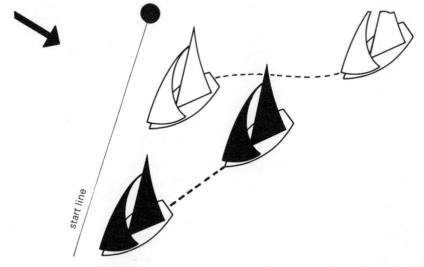

but this only works if Black does not choose to luff or is unable to because she is travelling too slowly.

Full speed in the right direction at the gun gives nearly half a length advantage over most helmsmen, for so many use the gun as a signal to sheet in and harden on to the wind. This hardening up to full speed close hauled has to happen at least five seconds before the gun and two lengths or more from the line for a crack start; it takes most dinghies about five seconds to gather maximum way from a standstill in medium weather.

Starting on an imaginary line, short of the real one, five seconds before the gun is the best way to be sure of crossing the true line with full speed at the gun. Half a length on the start line is usually worth at least 20 lengths at the finish.

Teamwork at the start
The emphasis so far has been on making the best individual start, no matter which team nearby boats belong to. Once good individual starting becomes more a routine than an event, then some attention can be given to starting in the position most likely to make things difficult for an opponent. There are several ways of ruining his start (this may sound harsh, but it is part of the game):

1 Give a close and powerful lee-bow. The position is established before the gun, the leeward boat luffs gently on its approach to close with an overtaking upwind opponent. She then goes for a good start and the upwind boat is in her lee-bow.
2 Force an upwind opponent over the line.

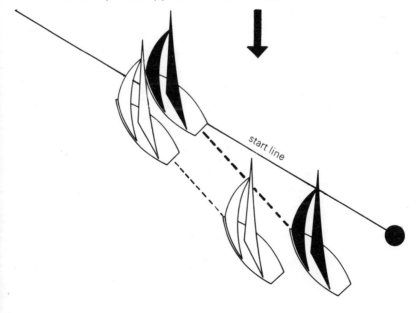

start line

This one requires accurate judgement and nerve. A faint-hearted attempt results in the upwind man remaining on the right side of the line to make an excellent start. Better for White also to be over with Black than have that happen.

3 Block the weather end on a biased line.

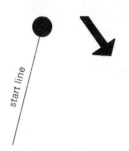

White travels slowly and passes the starboard distance mark close enough to deny Black entry. Black can do one of three things—wait for White to start and follow in her wake, sail the wrong side of the weather mark, or go for White's lee. Whatever Black does she has lost the initiative.

In each of these three examples, White's start is not seriously impaired. She upsets the opponent's start without damaging her own; she spoils the opposition, almost in passing, in the course of making a good start herself. The circumstances when she ought to sacrifice her own good start are rare and are discussed in chapter 8.

While opposition boats which come within range at the start can be hindered, teammates are to be avoided. To make a cracking start hard under the lee of a teammate is quite acceptable but the lee-bow should not be made to work. Instead of pinching, the leeward man sails a little freer off the line to give his teammate clear wind. It is better still to avoid a really close position with a teammate by altering course before the gun to give him room. Rather than leaving a team-mate to follow in line past the weather end of a biased line, dropping to leeward a little lets him in upwind and two thirds of the side start well.

However, starting well is difficult and a helmsman should not make concessions to teammates if by doing so his own start is ruined. Each man goes for the best individual start.

Reaching Starts

Reaches tend to be processions. As the order of the procession is set at the beginning of the leg a reaching start must be handled well.

The best position on the line in the absence of other boats is usually the nearest to the first mark (that is true on a reach, but *not* on a beat).

For instance:

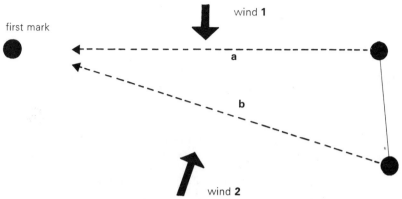

first mark

wind **1**

a

b

wind **2**

Course **a** obviously gives the shortest distance to the mark, and in wind direction 1 is also the fastest.

This is not always so for even though course **a** is the shorter, in planing conditions and wind direction 2 the broader reach provided by course **b** would give a faster ride to the mark. Yet in light winds from direction 2, course **a** is best. Each line must be assessed on its merits and the factors which can favour a start at the end further from the first mark are:

1 Faster point of sailing.
2 Tidal advantage.

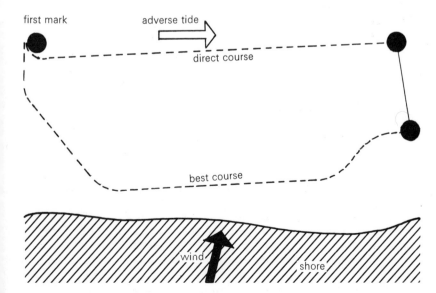

first mark

adverse tide

direct course

best course

wind

shore

3 Wind advantage created by the lie of the land.

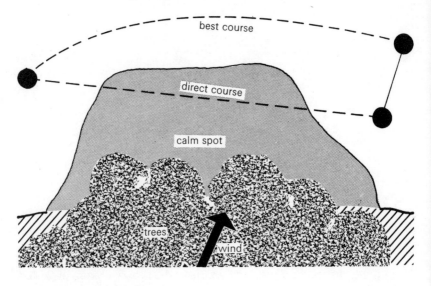

4 Wind flaws in light air.

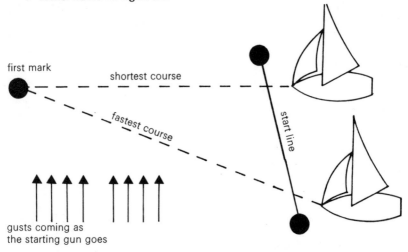

The windward boat takes the approaching gusts first and the resulting gain more than offsets the extra distance sailed.

Full speed on the line as the gun goes is vital to a good reaching start. A helmsman who can achieve this comes off the line with a clear advantage. Compare a boat making the ideal start with a boat which has made a slow approach and is still accelerating as the gun goes.

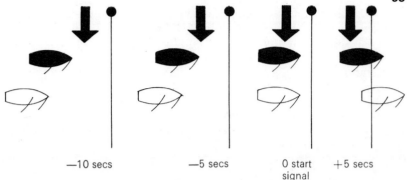

This looks well on paper, but to make so precise a start the skipper of the white boat has to judge his fast approach very finely. A late start lets Black away upwind while an early start and recall really costs ground. How can the white boat ride in at full speed and make the line within a second or two of the gun?

Once again, the starting method is more easily appreciated when the other boats are out of the picture.

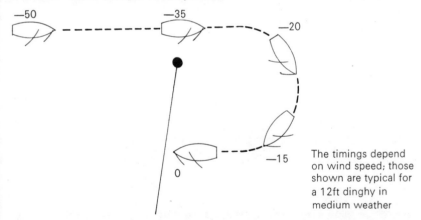

The timings depend on wind speed; those shown are typical for a 12ft dinghy in medium weather

The boat reaches towards the line, takes the time crossing in the wrong direction (say, 35 seconds), gybes with just less than half of the remaining time gone (20 seconds to go) and goes full tilt for the line to cross on the gun. Two or three practice runs give the timing, after these the final 10 or 15 seconds can be sailed confidently at full speed. Nearby boats interfere little with the timing unless severe avoiding action has to be taken.

Alternatively a slow timed run can be used so long as the final acceleration period is long enough to give full way at the starting gun—at least five seconds with most dinghies and more with the larger ones.

The boat should be far enough back from the line to give room to sail the last 5–15 seconds at full speed. This method is more flexible than the first but requires careful judgement; it is less of an exact starting formula.

A start in the middle of the line is difficult to judge without transits as there is no mark on the water by which to gauge the line's position. A shore transit with the committee boat (or a distance mark if it is near enough to the line) can be used here; the line's position is thus known accurately. The transit serves very well if a bunch gathers at the weather end.

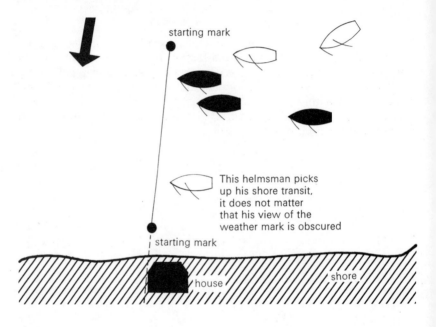

starting mark

This helmsman picks up his shore transit, it does not matter that his view of the weather mark is obscured

starting mark

house

shore

A fast leeward start can be made using the discovered shore transit to give complete confidence about the position of the line. Timed trial runs are valuable for trying out the transits which are to be used in the real start.

Clear wind is limited in a reaching start so the boats of a team must make the most of the available wind. This means spreading over the line. Only one boat can make the ideal start so it is futile for all three to go for it. Less favourable as it may be, a start to leeward of the bunch should be made by one man. His start may not pay on the face of it, but one boat is better to be sure of a good, unobstructed start giving, say, third place than dropping to sixth after losing out in the bunch. The team's start is then spread and teammates are not affecting each other with dirty wind as they draw away from the line.

A windward start sequence
The following sequence of pictures was taken at the final of the
Association of Northern Universities Sailing Clubs (ANUSC) 1969
championships. The competition was held in 420 dinghies. The start
line is marked by two buoys, one in the foreground and the other on
the left. Wind force 4. 25 seconds to the gun.

The helmsman of 5622 turns an eagle eye on 4919 and decides to
luff. 15 seconds to go:

5622 luffs but 4919 has not yet responded. The helmsman on the
extreme left has allowed himself to sail too far away from the line and
is having to plane back at top speed. 5620 is in danger of being early
so waits. 10 seconds to go:

5622 stops luffing and slacks off the jib to avoid being on the line too soon. The boat on the right is early and begins a gybe to come back on port tack late. If her helmsman had let both sails fly five seconds ago he would have made the line on time without having to throw away ground in a gybe. If letting the sails go had not slowed the boat enough, then backing the jib quickly would have done the trick. By resorting to the gybe he threw away the opportunity to make the start which 5622 finally made. Instead he starts last. 6 seconds to go:

5622 is going for the fast start at the port end, but her skipper is concerned about arriving too soon so the jib flaps. One second to go :

The boat on the left is going to be late but has at least a clear part of the line. Anxious faces look for the start signal. The gun goes.

A second later:

5622 makes a good start. To drive home her tactical advantage over 4919, she must pinch to make the lee bow work, all the time sailing as upright as possible to cast the biggest possible wind deflection to windward. If 5622 can make the lee bow work quickly, 4919 is in trouble because the boats upwind stop her tacking away for clear wind. The boat on the left is late but nevertheless makes a good start and will almost certainly be ahead of 4919 after 100 yards of clear-wind sailing.

With the positions at the beginning of the sequence identical but with 5622 and 4919 on the same team, the tactics of the helmsmen would have been quite different. Instead of luffing, 5622 would have sailed for the start she made without worrying about the boat upwind. 4919 would have deliberately slowed to let 5622 go clear away to leeward (she made a mistake by not doing this anyway). If the two were teammates and their positions on the line those of the last picture, the right thing for 5622 to do would be to sail as fast as possible, just a fraction free, so that the lee bow on her teammate did not take effect. 4919 meanwhile would pinch.

More About Beating Part 2

Slowing an opponent by close covering

Team racing, as we have already seen, demands strict covering on the beat, both as a form of defence against an opponent astern and a method of attack to slow a boat down. But used as a slowing device, normal covering is not particularly powerful because if the leading boat is sailing at full close hauled speed, the slowing effect on the boat she covers is negligible. The pursuer tends to tail the leader equally fast two or three lengths away; closer than this she is slowed by wind shadow, further away and the wind disturbance is minimal. So if the boat astern is to be held back, something more agressive is needed: the leading helmsman must slow his own boat while holding the opponent firmly in the centre of his wind shadow. Then the following boat will travel as slowly as the leader—provided she remains trapped in the turbulent wind.

There are two ways by which a helmsman can slow his boat on a normal close hauled course: by letting the jib fly or the mainsail flap. Either way the boat carries on in the same direction but at reduced speed. The idea is to cast the biggest possible wind shadow while still retaining complete control of the boat.

Compare the flow pattern picture of a sloop rig beating normally

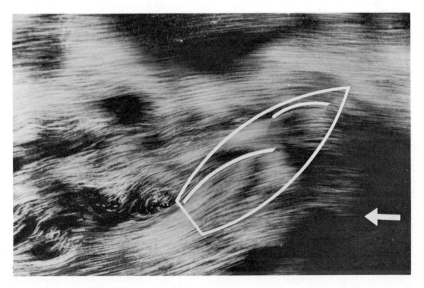

with that of a single sail set at the same angle.

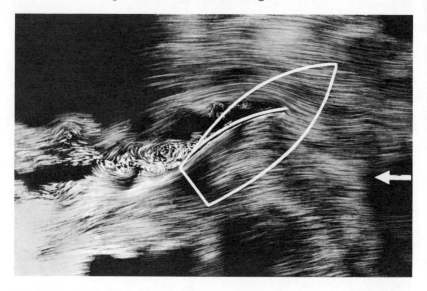

Without a jib there is no slot effect; flow breaks away sooner behind the mainsail and creates greater turbulence downwind.

Although a flapping jib looks as if it is carving up the wind more strongly than one drawing normally, in fact the energy taken from the wind—and consequently the slowing effect—is less. The result of letting the jib flap, as far as air flow is concerned, is to create greater turbulence from the mainsail but less from the jib. In many dinghies the reduction in boat speed is as much as one third.

Most experienced helmsmen slow the opposition by freeing the jib rather than the mainsail. There is a practical point in favour of this, for with the mainsail set normally inboard there is no boom or main-sheet trailing to leeward to be fouled by the other boat.

A more turbulent pattern can be created by sheeting the mainsail further in than usual when the jib is released. The flow pictures for mainsails at different angles of attack (p 91) show this.

Before describing the practical business of using the slowing method, a word of warning—and this goes for a good deal of what follows in this chapter. The technique will be new to anyone who has only previously competed in individual races, it is not easy and quite likely to fail at first. This is no reason immediately to write off the technique as impractical, because with a little perseverence anyone can make it work.

Before starting to slow the man behind, correct boat positions are vital for success: the downwind boat has to be placed right in the centre of your mainsail's wind shadow.

With the boats properly lined up White's helmsman begins the slowing manoeuvre by releasing his jib. He then concentrates on relative boat positions. The actual sailing of the boat has to be almost automatic, with all his attention reserved for the dinghy astern in an effort to hold her in the most turbulent wind between a half and one boat's length away. He has his crew harden or release the jib to vary the boat speed and continues to spill maximum dirty wind on target. Covering normally—

Covering with jib flapping.

If Black tries to drive out to leeward

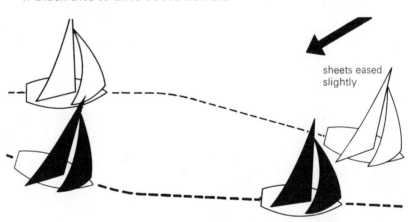

sheets eased slightly

White's crew pulls the jib in and the boat is sailed fast and a little free to regain the ideal position. With Black safely back in the right place White's jib is let fly and slowing begins again. The mainsail fills all the time to retain full control. Black's attempt to break clear could have succeeded if White had slowed too much; when it failed it cost ground to windward so White still achieved her aim—slowing Black. (White is allowed to free off—see page 128.)

In sailing to windward at something like two thirds the normal speed tacking is obviously impaired, which gives the pursuer some chance of breaking clear by putting in quick tacks at the right moments. The leading helmsman must therefore watch cat-like for any attempted escape by his prey. The secret of tacking well at reduced speed is a steady roll; a smooth, not too violent tack with both sails drawing immediately on rounding. Easing off a fraction free after the tack helps the boat to pick up maximum speed quickly and, in the case of the leader, to regain the ideal slowing position without delay. It is better to be in a commanding position slightly forward of the ideal, and drop back into it after the tack, than be too far back and allow the following boat any chance of breaking out to leeward.

So much for the man in the white boat who is doing the slowing manoeuvre, now to look at the duel from the point of view of the victim helming the black boat. If the leader knows what he is doing, and makes no mistake Black's predicament is unenviable—he either sails on regardless and is seriously slowed, or wriggles and tries everything to escape and slows himself. But the covering boat, however competently sailed, can sometimes be forced into error.

White, in enthusiasm to delay Black, may occasionally slow too much. When this happens, a quick tack by Black followed by fast and free sailing is likely to leave White, whose tack was slower, struggling to regain a covering position.

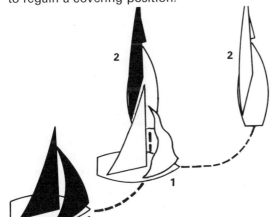

Black, with her jib clear now, has an opportunity of gaining clear wind by sailing faster, followed perhaps by a lee-bow position which would force White to tack away.

White may on the other hand fall back occasionally, which gives Black's helmsman a possible opening to leeward.

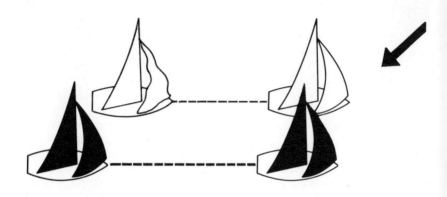

If the leeward break fails to work success might come from a tacking battle, when every trick in the book can be used to try and break cover. Although constant tacking will lose both boats ground, it does at least unsettle the slowing manoeuvre.

A danger in this sort of dog fight is that the rest of the race may go ignored. The second helmsman, for instance, is being slowed by White to finish behind another white boat, which means that if he occupies himself solely with the duel the second white boat is free to overtake, provided the slowing process works. On the other hand, if he covers White's teammate coming up astern all the slowing move will do is to bunch the boats together, not change their order.

The best defence for the victim is to cover the opponent immediately behind, for then there can be no order change. But even this defence fails if the leader covers so closely that the victim is unable to tack off without a collision.

Slowing by this method works best in medium weather when a boat can be held to about two thirds of its normal unobstructed sailing speed. With practice, you can gain enough confidence in your ability to slow someone down that you can use the method not only to win a match which would otherwise be lost, but also to increase a lead.

In the following pair of pictures the boat with dark patches on both sides of her bow is on one team and the remaining three are on the other. The leg is a beat.

The boat with the patch is about to be slowed by the boat on the right, waiting to lee bow her, and the one on the left, reaching down to close up and spill maximum dirty wind. Notice that both helmsmen doing the slowing manoeuvre are concentrating entirely on the boat to be slowed, the sailing of their own boats being less important than correct positioning in relation to their opponent.

Now the third member of the team does exactly the right thing: tacks off into clear wind. The boat with the patch is in trouble now. She is being slowed by the boat on the left and, because of her closeness, is unable to tack to cover the boat behind which is going about. If the boat on the left now slows her opponent down by keeping him in wind shadow and letting the jib flap, her teammate who is tacking off in clear wind should cross them both when they meet again, thereby dropping the boat with the patch to the back of the group. The team without patches thus gain one place.

66

Slowing an opponent by lee-bowing

Although the use of the lee-bow position is limited to situations where the opponent is unable or unwilling to tack away to escape, it can be a powerful slowing weapon. To make it so, the overlap has to be maintained and the windward boat, Black, luffed virtually to a standstill. (Diagram on page 18.)

White's helmsman drops back a little to give Black the windward overlap and then pinches hard and persistently. Throughout, he hardens or releases the jib as necessary to hold Black overlapped. If Black tacks off White can tack too and hold Black on a completely wasteful overstanding tack.

The lee-bow influence can be increased by the leeward yacht if she heels to windward. Not only is the windward heel more effective from an aerodynamic point of view but it also brings the rig of the boat (particularly higher up) further upwind. The result is a stronger lee-bow (that is a bigger deflection of the wind) and one which extends further, so the leeward boat can usefully heel to windward.

The weather boat, by doing the same, can draw her rig away from the area of strongest backwinding. Therefore both boats have an incentive to heel to windward: one to spread the area of backwinding, the other to strike for clearer air with the higher part of the rig.

At the windward mark

The first boat to the weather mark does not necessarily lead away from it if an opponent is close behind. The usual sequence is:

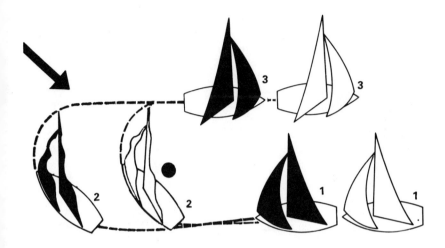

Unable to tack in White's water, Black stands on and allows White to round first. To be sure of forcing Black past the mark, White must be close on her transom and travelling at least as fast. Then, if Black looks like going about, a call by the helmsman of the white boat of 'Don't tack in my water' usually removes any thought his adversary might have about chancing his arm and tacking.

But the leading helmsman can hold his place if he acts in time. As he approaches the mark and the bow of his boat comes within the two length circle he pinches with sheets eased a little and slows down.

White, carrying more way, overtakes either to windward or leeward. She has no right to water at the mark to windward of Black, and if she elects to go to leeward Black has the inside berth at the mark and is entitled to call for water and tack.

So all the leader has to do to safeguard his position is to pinch and slow, or simply slow by easing sheets, to force the following boat into an outside overlap. He can equally well gain his freedom to tack by luffing fairly hard immediately before going about.

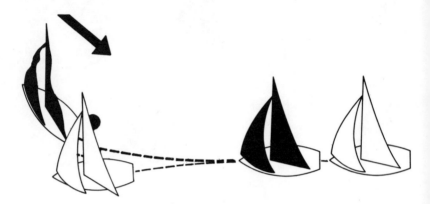

So much for Black's escape, but the helmsman of White need not let her get away so easily. He simply slows when Black slows and refuses to be forced outside, all the time remaining close enough to Black's transom to prevent her from tacking. The winner in this little encounter is the man who best uses his wits and judgement—but with the odds in the leader's favour.

Another situation in which places change arises at a weather mark.

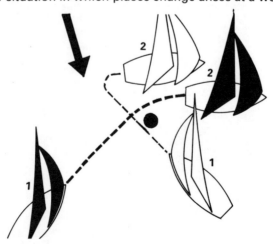

Although White sails in here with starboard rights, Black will lead away from the mark because White cannot tack immediately.

But White can hold onto her lead if she slows before reaching the mark to set up this position:

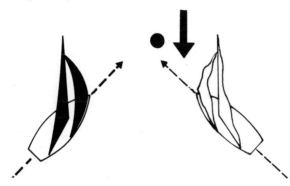

Now Black has a choice between bearing away under White's stern and failing to lay the mark, or tacking onto starboard to avoid a collision. Black's defence here is, as before, to slow so that White fails to force her into tacking. Again, the winner is the best judge of how much speed to lose. (See rule on page 129.)

Forcing a boat to overstand a weather mark
Although the ideal sailing-on position does sometimes arise by chance it can also be set up.

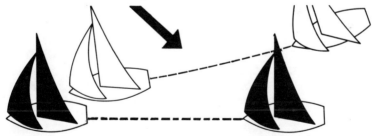

By sacrificing ground to windward, White makes it impossible for Black to tack and clear her stern. Black can only escape now if her helmsman takes some decisive action—the alternative is to sail on until either White goes about or they reach the shore. The defences open to Black are:

1 Pinch hard to make the lee-bowing position work—effective when the boats are close together or in line astern, but it takes time to climb into a position from which a tack is possible, and this time is lengthened when White also pinches.
2 Slow down, bear away and tack clear of White's stern.

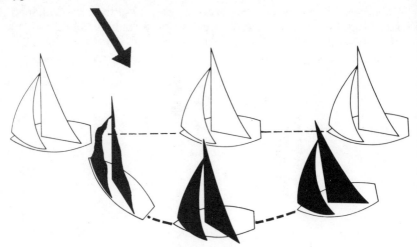

The least wasteful way out if pinching does not work quickly. But again, if White's skipper is intent on stopping the escape he too can slow down and bear off—stalemate with White gaining time.

3 Gybe.

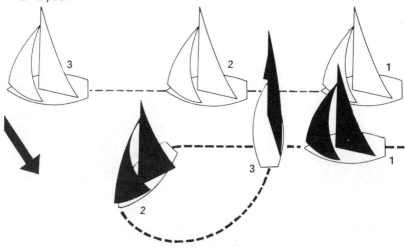

The most wasteful escape, but at least White has no way of blocking it.

Slowing a nearby boat from behind

The usual way to delay a boat ahead which is close covering is to throw a series of tacks in quick succession.

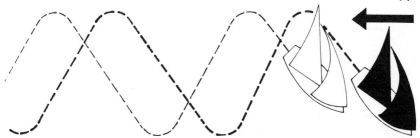

This ploy works perfectly well in most conditions and against most opposition, but it falls down in shifting winds against good helmsmen. The leader, as soon as he realises what is happening, can stay on a lifting shift when the boat he is covering tacks off, with the result that he has gained several lengths by the time they meet again and his pursuer no longer has the power to force him into a series of wasteful tacks. To avoid this, but still hold back the leading boat, White's helmsman has to be more subtle, not forcing the issue quite so strongly.

Instead of trying to hold up Black in a tacking duel, White's skipper can make her sail the beat badly by drawing her off to an unfavourable part of the leg: into a calm, the lee of trees, adverse tide or perhaps the wrong way up a systematic wind shift. The advantage here lies in the time it takes before Black's helmsman realises he is being taken for a ride. When he does, both boats will have travelled far enough from the rest of the fleet to make recovery difficult or impossible. His dilemma then is unenviable: either to safeguard himself against White and let another attacker pass, or to break away from White when it is perhaps too late to hold off the other opponent anyway. So White can force Black's helmsman into a losing situation before he realises what is happening or can do much to recover, and another white boat overtakes them both.

The covered boat here, 480, can dictate the tactics of 248 and, if necessary, make her sail the slowest route to the weather mark.

Another way to hold up an adversary who is covering you is to take the wrong shifts. Each time you are lifted tack, then he tacks to cover. Because you tack on the lifts instead of the headers, the tacks you take are the wrong ones and you sail further to the weather mark— and so does the man ahead. This may appear an unlikely way of slowing him down since he can simply refuse to be enticed away on bad shifts. But if the following boat is not tacking too often the leader will usually cover.

This method works less well when the boats are some distance apart. The man ahead gets the favourable lift first and uses it for a few moments before it reaches the pursuer, so each time the pursuer tacks on a lift the leader has an advantage which depends on the time the lift takes to reach the following boat. Therefore when the boats are close together the method works, but when further apart the following boat does better to take the good shifts in order to close within two or three lengths of the leader and then lead him away on the wrong shifts.

Making an opponent take the tacks you want him to
In all the covering situations dealt with so far the tactics have been dictated by the following boat, unless the leader was prepared to take a chance and leave his pursuer to go off unattended. Ideally the leader would like to keep the boat behind covered, but at the same time choose which tacks he wants to take. To have such power over the boat behind is clearly asking too much, but he can go quite a long way towards sailing the race as he wants while keeping approximately between the pursuing boat and the weather mark.

A good covering tack exactly on the wind of an opponent usually causes a reflex response in him to tack away. On the other hand a bad cover tack allows him clear wind, a small psychological victory and

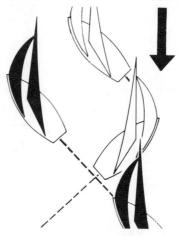

as likely as not Black will hold on. Apart from the almost clear wind he now enjoys there is a chance of his breaking out to leeward and lee-bowing White so he remains on starboard tack.

The helmsman of Firefly 2383, by leaving 3315 clear wind, encourages her to remain on port tack.

White's helmsman in the previous diagram may want to take the port tack ; then it would be chancy to leave Black on starboard. This time the first tack comes exactly on Black's wind to persuade her to tack. She goes about and Black tacks.

White's final covering tack back onto port is left late to give Black the smell of a leeward break in clear air. If Black goes about again onto starboard, White tacks exactly on her wind to encourage her back onto the desired port tack—in this way White biases the beat all the time towards the port tack.

The windward dinghy has a fair degree of control over the leeward one, for by sailing a little faster and freer she can take up the ideal covering position.

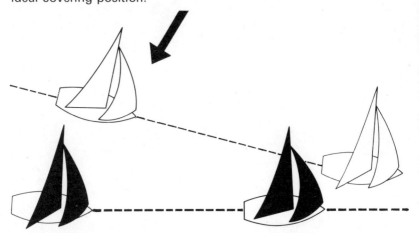

The black boat will probably tack when this happens. White has control of the situation, a fact which Black's helmsman will probably not realise if he is unfamiliar with the technique. He takes it on face value, as a normal covering episode.

Flirting with Black's leeward opening in this way is a risky business. Before White's skipper makes his decision to influence the direction of Black's beat he should weigh up the factors which could throw things out of his control.

1 A long leg gives the leeward boat, Black, the opportunity to make a lee-bow work.
2 An opponent on White's wind gives the leeward boat her chance to pull out ahead while White sails in dirty wind. White's helmsman therefore has to look at all his opponents' placings carefully before starting the manoeuvre.
3 If the leeward boat has been footing particularly fast she may break clear, even on a fairly short tack.

Practice The incentive to do well in races makes them a bad experimental ground. A helmsman sails a race as fast as he can. He might know, for example, that roll tacking is better than his own method of going about, but before his tacking improves it will get worse while he is finding out what a roll tack is all about. If he tries to roll tack in the course of a race he finds it inefficient, and so rejects it and reverts to his usual method. The same learning process applies to improving most of the elements of good helmsmanship: rounding marks, gybing and handling gusts for example. An hour or two sailing around trying different things does more for helming skill than five times as long in a race repeating procedures which were quite often learned incorrectly in the first place. The knowledge of a boat and how she handles come so much more quickly after sailing her without a rudder for instance, or sailing backwards on purpose. If you can handle a force 7 in practice—where your only adversaries are the natural conditions—you can race that much more easily in a force 6. No longer is it quite the same battle for survival, you can get down to racing with greater confidence and can think more about boat speed and tactics.

Equally, many of the manoeuvres described in this chapter are techniques of helmsmanship and—like other techniques—improve with practice. To imagine that after reading how to slow a boat to windward you can make the manoeuvre work in a race straightaway is to look for failure. This and several other techniques are difficult and quite outside normal individual racing; the ability to use them efficiently in a team race depends on the sort of confidence which comes by practising. The more efficiently they are used the better and more rewarding the team race is likely to be.

One way of practising which brings in slowing methods is to sail with two teams of two boats a side. The side whose boat finishes third wins. This rather devious method of deciding the winner proves a tremendous incentive to slow opposition boats. Take, for instance, a winning combination for White.

For Black to take the lead the leading boat A must drop P to last when the order becomes:

Now it is the white boat Q's turn to slow a black boat and so it continues. The essence of the game is to go as slowly as possible while at the same time keeping one opposition boat astern. As a method of practising it can be quite instructive because it emphasises so strongly the role of slowing techniques.

This pattern of racing is not a very satisfactory one for matches because the ability to sail fast counts for nothing : the result depends solely on slowing ability. But two a side can work particularly well in races if the method of deciding the winner is different. First place home is no use because then the race is entirely for first place, but if the team with last place loses things are much more entertaining.

If one team sails away 1 and 2 they deservedly win. If they hold places 1 and 4 they lose and have to do something between them to lift 4 up the fleet and leave the opposing side in the defeat position. The answer is for 1 to slow an opponent into last place. As a form of racing the system works extremely well and can, incidentally, be used in a best of three series if someone fails to turn up for a normal three-a-side match.

Once you have learnt the basic slowing skills by practising with the 'third place loses' system there is no need to use it thereafter. The 'last place loses' system introduces a much broader range of tactics and is ideal for learning very quickly just how effective team tactics can be. For team racing within a club, and for learning how to think in terms of a team, this system is excellent.

Looking at the team as a whole While practice outside races helps to perfect manoeuvres directed against one other boat, tactics concerning the whole team can only be learned in races. The ideas and the logic behind the sport are certainly important and can be absorbed ashore—after all the point of this book is to give some background knowledge which will help to solve actual race problems—but this knowledge alone is quite useless unless it is applied on the water. This can only happen given enough team races to sail during a season to find out, in practical terms, precisely what the unfamiliar techniques and tactics are all about.

It is no use knowing why a cover tack placed late should drive an opponent in the desired direction if, every time the move is tried, he drives out to leeward and gains a lee-bowing position. With simple manoeuvres there are right and wrong ways of doing things, but once we leave the basic principles dealt with in chapter 3, tactics are less clear cut. What follows now is therefore an attempt to give some further ideas on team race thinking rather than lay down hard and fast rules about what to do in set situations.

Quick thinking Events sometimes follow one another with such startling speed in races that you can easily find yourself overtaken by their sheer pace; then decisions are forced on you rather than made. Relieved of the helm, perhaps sitting on the shore watching a race, it is easy to see exactly what everyone ought to be doing, and a simple matter to pick out their mistakes.

But on the water you would probably make the same errors yourself.

In the club bar after a match it is usually easy to see, when discussing with teammates, exactly what the mistakes were and how they could have been avoided—this is also the best way to improve tactics. The race can be frozen and, given time, the right answers come out. On the water you can not hold up your hand and shout 'Stop' as soon as everything starts happening quickly (not with any hope of success anyhow), but you can win time in another way: by making decisions sooner.

A good tactician remains exasperatingly cool even when things are happening so quickly that he ought to be flustered, and whatever surprises the opposition may spring he responds quickly and decisively. The reason is simply that there are only a limited number of moves that the opposition can make, all of them identifiable, and our tactician friend has every possible move worked out and a decision made for each before it happens. So he wins time by making his decisions some time before he needs them, and many of them are not used at all because the opposition just do not make those moves. This contingency planning is rather wasteful—making up your mind about things that never happen in the end—but at least with those that do happen you know exactly what you are going to do.

The sort of questions to be asking yourself in the course of a race are: 'If the boat four lengths to leeward tacks and everyone else stays on their present tack what is my best move, do I hold on or tack?' 'Another opposition man is about to cross behind, if my teammate to leeward does not cover shall I?. . .' And so on—with answers of course. To think about the race in this way means that the actual business of helming the boat fast has to be almost second nature—like driving down the M1 concentrating on a radio play. This is why you need to have a reasonably good standard of helmsmanship before you can get the most out of team racing.

Defending a points lead The best way to hold on to a points lead is to gain places, either by simply sailing faster than the other side or by using team racing strategy to bring teammates up from behind. Speed is always the aim unless some team race delaying manoeuvre is called for. When do the leaders need to use these manoeuvres? In the first place the underdogs are likely to want close tactics as they have most to gain by them: the race leaders have no reason to entangle with the other side voluntarily as they are winning anyway. Safe-guarding the position has to be the aim. So before anyone on the leading side decides to hold back an opponent he has to be nearly certain that he is not going to lose out in the involvement. The safest techniques—sailing a boat to overstand a mark or, close covering—are the best ones to use, and then only in the right situation.

A model of safe slowing when leading is the incident described in Chapter 3 when a West Kirby helmsman sailed an opponent past the weather mark to let his teammates past into first and second places—safe and devastating.

The most uncomfortable time for the race leaders is when, in a delicately balanced match, one of their own men is threatened by two opponents astern. Rigid defence by covering is no longer any use as one cannot cover two. Take, for instance, a winning 1, 3, 6 combination. White lead by $9\frac{3}{4}$ points to 11.

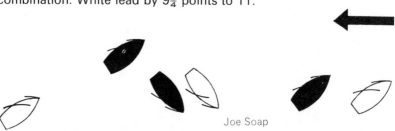

Joe Soap

Joe Soap lying third is in the hot seat with two opponents close behind. If he covers one a tacking battle starts, the other overtakes and the place by which his team leads is lost. In the first race of a two race match the answer is usually to play safe; cover one, leave the other alone and accept a three quarter point deficit carried to the second race. But in the second race, a critical place threatened in this way is best defended by loose covering only, by taking more notice of wind shifts and boat speed than of the pursuers. The difficulty is less if one of the challengers is appreciably slower than the other, for then covering can be concentrated on the fast one, only to be broken off if a short tacking battle or an unfavourable tack threatens to allow the slow man through.

A short tacking battle can be stopped by the defender in two ways: by tacking more efficiently than the other boat, which then loses ground on each tack,

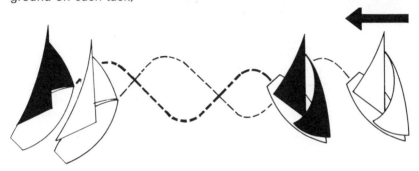

or by refusing to be drawn onto a bad windshift.

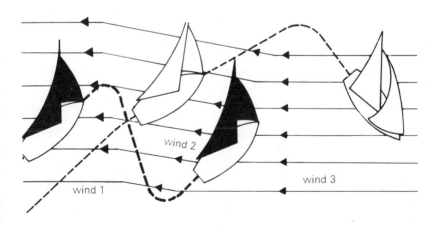

In each case the heat is taken out of the battle; the pursuer no longer has as strong a hand to play once White gains a psychological victory.

If Joe Soap has just a slight edge of speed and the courage, his best bet is probably to persuade one of the men behind to go in the direction he wants him to by placing the covering tack late. In this way he may be able to keep the pair of them reasonably well together.

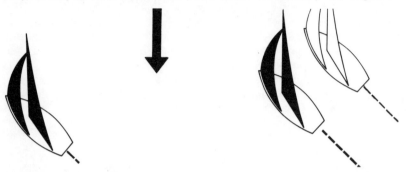

Joe now manages to move much more in line between his opponents and the windward mark, thereby reducing his chances of being passed. (This ploy incidentally, often works well on the last beat of an individual race). Equally, the method can be used to persuade the pursuing boat to stay on a chosen windshift.

If all this fails and White lose the one vital place on which the match depends, what can Joe Soap do to recover? There is no need to attempt to gain the position that has just been lost by fast sailing, that would be far too difficult. Instead, he concentrates on the man behind, and by slowing, drops him behind the following white boat into last place.

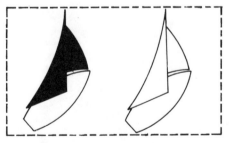

The points here referred to a single race for simplicity. The positions would be different but the principle the same in the second race of an evenly balanced match.

The cut and dried win-lose concept applies only to the second race of a two race match, and for the purpose of deciding tactical policy the first is better considered as incomplete at the finish. Every place counts of course, but when losing in the first race, particularly by a small margin, making up a points deficit is not critical to winning the match; in the second race it is.

A first race can therefore be sailed more conservatively than the second: more guarded in defence and less riskily aggressive in attack. The exception is a disastrous start, 4, 5, 6 say, when the underdogs have to try everything reasonable and legal to gain a score with which they can enter the second race having some hope of success. The second race tends to be more exciting. Everyone knows which finishing positions spell a win and they go onto the water intent on gaining them: the defence and attack approach then has a very marked effect on the tactics.

When a leading team successfully counters every move made against them the losing side inevitably lose some of their fight and become dispirited. The leaders' position is safer if they have this psychological upper hand. Good teamwork contributes more to this than anything, but there are a few tactical refinements which also help to demoralise the losing side.

Take the crossing of two beating boats for example. White lead and the white boat is about to cover the black one. The usual sequence of events is:

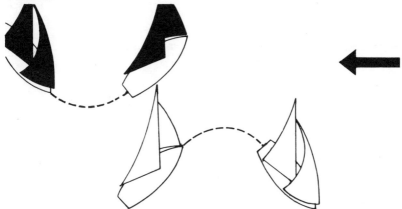

White puts in a covering tack which forces Black to tack off and clear her wind. They separate. For White to stay with Black and cover her, the covering tack would come a little later.

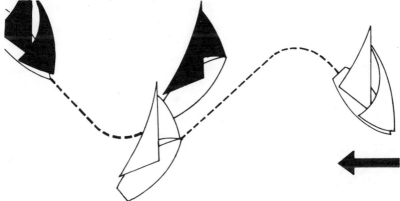

Now Black either holds on and goes for the leeward break or tacks as White tacks. If Black tacks, White can make a second tack upwind and by easing sheets a fraction after the tack, sail fast and free to take up a covering position on Black's wind.

It is dangerous to make the second tack too soon after the first since the boat needs two or three lengths in which to pick up way after going about. A following helmsman, in the effort to overtake, frequently throws a couple of tacks in very quick succession; the leader gains by staying calm and making quite certain that he has full way on the boat before going into the second tack.

Occasionally this one comes off:

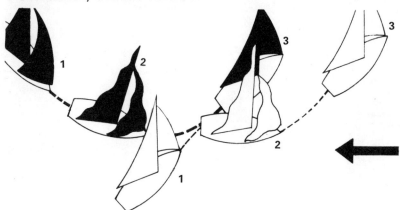

Black's helmsman expects White to cover in the usual way, and not for a moment expecting White's dummy tacks straight into her wind shadow. The black boat is hardly likely to show her best form for a few minutes after this.

Situations that crop up while team racing sometimes provide scope for the talents of the more ingenious tactician. For instance, when two boats approach a mark like this:

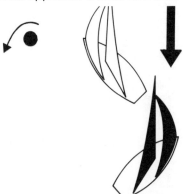

The following boat is inclined to use the course of the leader as a guide for laying the mark. If the leader is laying the mark comfortably he can take advantage of Black's attention; he simply bears away with both sails in the normal beating position to give the impression of being headed.

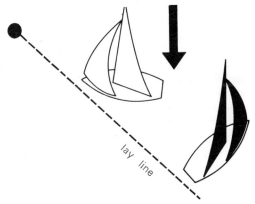

The following helmsman, seeing what he thinks is a header, sails well past the lay line and tacks while the leader heads up and rounds the mark a few lengths to the good.

Not the sort of thing you would do at every windward mark, but this type of bluff can be used occasionally in keen competition where experienced helmsmen are trying to outdo each other in boats of equal speed. Notice that this ploy can work only against good helmsmen; the man behind has to be thinking enough to use the leading boat as a pointer to wind direction. This sort of move and some of those described earlier—slowing to avoid tacking in water, dummy tacks for example—are the product of really keen racing. None of them were thought out ashore, each just happened in races when someone was really intent on winning.

Coming through to win from behind
Now to look at the problem from the other side, what can the losers do to save the match? Their problem is less if the three helmsmen are conversant with the various slowing techniques, certainly the more important ones, and sail no slower than the leaders. Then, if they are in contact with the other side, there is a good deal they can do. Because the leaders are almost certain to cover attentively, each covered boat dictates the tactics of the boat ahead—when the pursuer tacks the other follows—so the team which is behind has a big say in the tactics of the leaders, and they have to use this to undermine the leaders' position.

If everyone in the losing team keeps up constant pressure, someone on the other side will almost certainly make a mistake and drop a place. Once this happens, the losing team can often reap the benefit of their psychological dominance and gain more places. However improbable victory may seem at first, any match is far from lost until the finish, because once the leaders begin to falter there is a chance to break through—the London v O & C S S match described in Chapter 3 is all the evidence anyone could look for on that point.

Above all the pressure from behind must be kept up; the leaders deserve no peace and they have to be harassed as much as possible without abusing or misusing the rules. Tacking battles, forcing them to overstand marks, slowing by covering, leading them to the slowest part of a beat and any of the other methods described so far can be used to break their hold on the race. If you also make your calls confidently and pass really close to opposition rudders when beating on opposite tacks, your opponents get the idea that you really intend to win, which helps to upset their confidence.

But sharpness can be, and with some teams is, taken too far. It is possible to win a race sometimes by contriving an incident on the water that goes to protest and, by being sufficiently untruthful in the protest, win the decision and the race. In team racing there are frequent opportunities for close conflict between boats and for helmsmen to become aggressive and display the worst sides of themselves —however amiable they may manage to be ashore. When simple honesty between people is sacrificed in the interests of success there is just no point in racing—it is supposed to be pleasure, not business. A few years ago some of the top-level team racing was marred by a 'win-at-all-costs' attitude but fortunately the sport—in Britain anyway—seems to have largely passed through this uncomfortable adolescence.

Some unusual and entertaining tactics have also been used to rescue a losing side. On a short course of three rounds one losing side found itself in positions 2, 3, 6 with the leader clear away and their own last man hopelessly behind after a capsize. One race only and little prospect of them winning, either the leader had to be caught or the last man had to overtake the nearest opponent nearly a lap ahead. Little prospect, that is, until he waited for the race leader to come round one lap ahead, close covered him with the jib released to slow and dropped him behind both teammates.

This team therefore won with positions 1, 2, 6, the fact of 6 finishing a lap behind not affecting the points. The action of boat number 6 was controversial, but the RYA when questioned about the incident, answered that the boat which waited was on the same leg of the course and therefore entitled to interfere, despite being a lap behind. They have since reversed their decision and the ploy is now illegal.

Highly improbable tactics can occasionally work. Among the

most successful was a piece of gamesmanship tried by Bill Brock-bank of Hollingworth Lake SC. After rounding the first mark in the lead with the whole of the opposing team hot on his transom and his teammates fifth and sixth, he deliberately sailed for the wrong mark. The opposition—still extremely close—followed, more intent on overtaking him than watching where they were going. The last two Hollingworth boats sailed into unassailable first and second places before the gaggle returned to the correct course.

A variant of the same theme was used by Jeremy Pudney in an International 14 race. Instead of sailing off in the wrong direction he rounded the first mark the wrong way and each member of the opposing team followed—as did chaos when they attempted to unwind. Spectacular if it works, but you can look unusually foolish if it doesn't.

These extreme tactics are the exceptions. Most team races are won by using the less startling team tactics and by sailing fast, as the following account shows. The race was between London Corinthian and Castaways.

The match was decided on two races and the scores were added together. The start of the first race went badly for Castaways and they rounded the first mark 4, 5, 6. After a mile long run Jeremy Vines of Castaways succeeded in gaining an overlap on the last London Corinthian boat. Once he had the overlap he realised that he could probably let his teammates through.

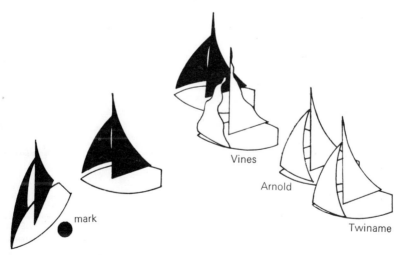

mark

Vines

Arnold

Twiname

By slowing about a boat's length in this position he also allowed the other two Castaways boats an overlap while still retaining the overlap on the opponent outside. This opponent was forced to round on the outside and dropped to last position. So at the leeward rounding Castaways lay 3, 4, 5 with Corinthian 1, 2, 6—

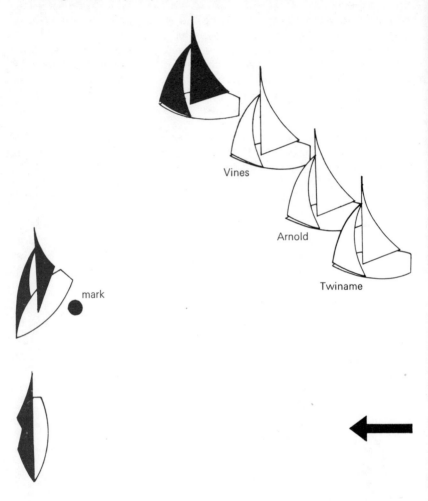

Vines

Arnold

Twiname

mark

On the next windward leg Eric Twiname tailed the second Corinthian boat and forced her to stay on one long tack in a shifting wind while Mike Arnold took advantage of the shifts and overtook both. Arnold then covered the Corinthian boat to let Twiname past as well. At the start of the final beat Castaways were placed 2, 3, 5 which gave them a lead of three quarters of a point.

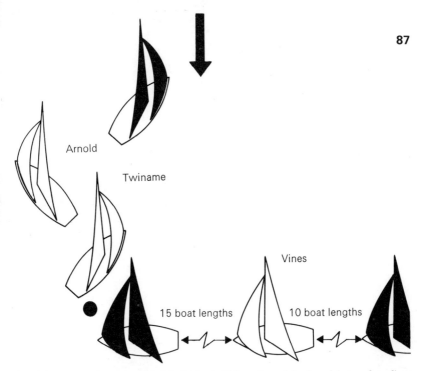

Arnold

Twiname

Vines

15 boat lengths 10 boat lengths

At this stage it was decided that Mike Arnold should try for first place while Twiname attempted to drop the second Corinthian man behind Jeremy Vines, by now about 70 yards astern.

Twiname began close covering the Corinthian boat with his jib released, and a tense duel began. The Corinthian helmsman short tacked, threw dummy tacks and tried everything to break cover and twice almost succeded. Meanwhile Vines closed from astern and a few lengths short of the finish line overtook to gain third place. Up front Arnold broke through the cover of the leading Corinthian helmsman just short of the line to take first place. Castaways finished 1, 3, 4.

This was hardly a typical team race because one team improved its position steadily throughout. Usually, team races are much more see-saw affairs than this with gains being made by each side at different times. Here and in the London v O & C S S race one team did everything right while the other made mistakes—not covering, or letting a tactical advantage slip. If the good tactics and the mistakes had come from both teams in the two race examples, the picture would have been more realistic but on the pages of a book less clear to follow. Team tactics are certainly very effective, but not always as consistently so as those two races would have it seem. Nevertheless in the second race of the Corinthian-Castaways encounter the match went to Corinthian, so there too the pendulum swung.

Downwind Part 2

The Reach

Slowing a boat by luffing
A good luff is an effective method of slowing down a nearby boat but it is difficult to do and can easily misfire. In the first place the victim has to be close upwind and overlapped before the luff begins.

If the black boat is too far back when the luff starts she can dip through to leeward; too far forward and the luff is curtailed by a mast abeam call. The windward dinghy is unlikely to place herself in exactly the position for a luffing match if she is expecting one so she must be taken by surprise. An appearance of unconcern and even nonchalance in the boat ahead often encourages the following helmsman to be bold, bold enough anyway to think that he can pass to windward. This is where he is going to be mistaken, but he must be as long as possible in discovering his error. When Black is in the right place to be luffed, the leeward yacht luffs decisively to the ideal position, a lee-bow.

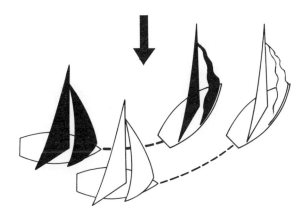

Black is now in the power of White's helmsman, who can hold her above the course as long as necessary. He does this by regulating the speed of his boat so that Black cannot drop back and slip round the stern; if Black slows, so must White to hold the position. Now

White pinches hard and not only takes Black off in the wrong direction but reduces her speed as well. There is a danger here which White's helmsman ought to look out for: a long climb out to windward on the reach may result in a run or broad reach to the next mark.

On the run Black has the opportunity to blanket White and gain the inside berth at the mark. The best way for White to avoid this is deliberately to give Black the opportunity to slip round her stern when the engagement has gone on long enough.

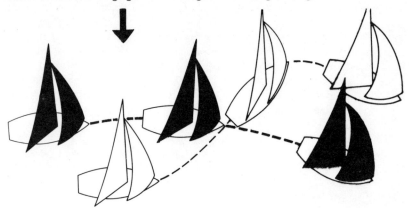

A particularly sharp final luff by White from which Black is just able to escape usually does the trick and Black faces the outside berth at the mark. White keeps a careful watch on the rest of the fleet as the object is to drop Black behind a teammate's boat, but not to let an opponent through as well.

The luff cannot be started at all if the black boat follows on the reach at the same speed. She may not oblige by starting to overtake, so she must be made to. White waits.

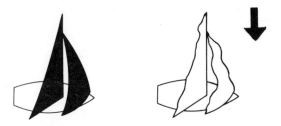

There is no surprise here, Black's helmsman knows White is out to fix him. He would be foolish to try and overtake to windward unless he has good reason for thinking he can break through on that side. Nevertheless Black's skipper may go to windward, and then a luffing match would start; but more likely he would go for White's lee.

Slowing an opponent by blanketing him

Black is still to be slowed even though she is to leeward. How can this be done?

The method of slowing a leeward boat is less spectacular than luffing but, properly handled, just as effective. The windward boat has first use of the wind. So if her wind shadow can be made to move a little slower than normal reaching speed a tantalising barrier is created which nearby downwind yachts will find it difficult to penetrate. The wind pattern round a normal reaching rig is:

with mainsail hardened to slow the boat the picture is:

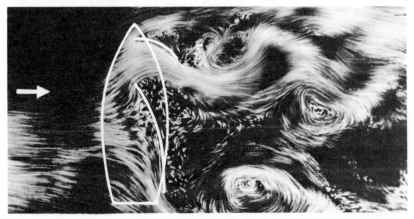

To prevent a downwind boat overtaking then, the mainsail should be hardened as this creates the maximum wind disturbance and a boat within two or three lengths to leeward is seriously affected. The rig is best held upright with the jib set for normal reaching. To safeguard against the leeward boat breaking through, the speeds of both boats must be similar when slowing begins. The method works most effectively on a beam reach, when a leeward boat can be kept to about three quarters of her clear wind speed.

Firefly 3315 was slowed so severely here that whenever she came too close to the other boat her mainsail completely lost the wind.

In gusty conditons the wind shadow can be used most powerfully as the gust strikes; the leeward boat is prevented from accelerating because the wind she has to sail in is highly confused. An overlap can be broken in this way.

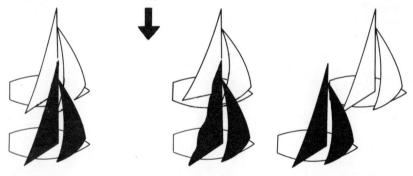

If White continues, Black looks like taking the inside overlap. To prevent this White slows allowing Black to come alongside to leeward, then hardens her mainsail, preferably at the beginning of a gust. Black flounders in turbulent wind and the overlap is broken. The technique is best used near a mark; the leeward boat is necessarily very close and once her overlap is broken there is little opportunity to establish it again. You can slow the opposition quite well on a reach, but you need to think carefully before slowing techniques are to be used. The decision depends on

    1 How desperate the situation is.

    2 How confident you are about succeeding in the slowing operation.

Opponents can only be slowed with small risk of the attempt failing if the two slowing techniques described are practised until they can be handled confidently. So given a better than even chance of succeeding a helmsman still has to decide when a slowing operation is called for. Dropping a boat back on the windward leg is less risky, so in the middle of a race delaying manoeuvres are generally best deferred until the beat. There are times, though, when a position can be more safely improved on the reach than elsewhere—usually when the pursuer is too close to be covered on the next beat.

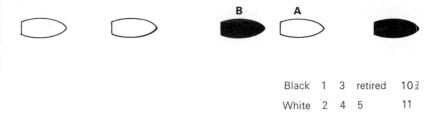

Black	1	3	retired	10¾
White	2	4	5	11

If this order is allowed to remain until the start of the beat, black boat B has an opportunity to tack off in clear wind and elude all white boats by sailing fast. To prevent this, White A forces her back into the middle of the white fleet. Even if B overtakes A in the process it does not matter because another white boat has overtaken them both.

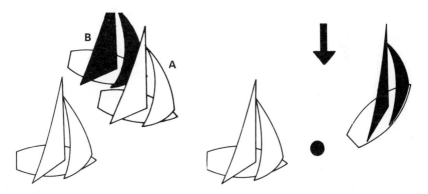

White is now better placed to drop Black to fifth and take a good points lead. The success of the slowing part of the manoeuvre can almost be guaranteed with only a little experience, but it is the recovery afterwards by the boat carrying it out that is less certain. So when there is still some distance to sail in a race, a helmsman who considers slowing has to think of the consequences if he fails to recover.

Positions which can be improved by slowing on a final reach are more straightforward: if the race is the first of two then the last reach is not the last of the match, and decisions should be made as though sailing in the middle of a race. Where the reaching leg of the final race is sailed directly to the finish line the underdogs should try extreme slowing tactics if there is the remotest chance of winning.

Luffing someone the wrong side of a mark
An opponent can be luffed the wrong side of a mark on a reach or a beat. The manoeuvre is an extreme and difficult one but can be very successful. The victim must be hailed before the leader's bow reaches the two length circle round the mark, otherwise the leader can be disqualified. Both then go the wrong side of the mark.

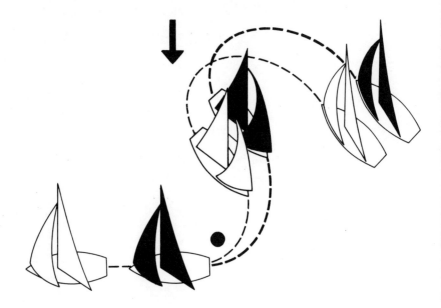

This manoeuvre serves two purposes: the obvious one of losing ground to allow teammates to gain, and the immediate benefit to the leader of breaking an overlap. The boat which luffs has to be sure of getting back to the mark ahead of the other. This is tricky if he has not gone wide enough to enable him to make an easy return, too close upwind of the mark and he has to spin too sharply and then the following boat may well then round ahead. In the heat of the luffing match boats which have already gone.round the mark can be a big collision risk.

The leader must sail past the mark for the manoeuvre to satisfy the rules (discussed on page 123).

Waiting to luff someone the wrong side of a mark
The white boat hovers stationary with her bow inside the two length circle.

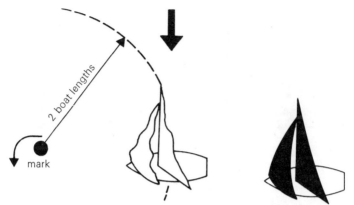

The helmsman of the approaching black boat has a problem. If he goes to leeward he is barging, so that if the white boat hits him as she bears away to round he is out; on the other hand an attempt to pass to windward invites a strong luff.

White's team would usually be in a pretty desperate position before this one was tried. The manoeuvre is precarious for White's skipper because he must stop with his bow inside the two length circle—and that is about as easy as standing still on a bicycle.

The black boat, then, is forced to go to windward if she is to stay in the race. Her helmsman's aim is to draw White upwind and clear of the two length circle.

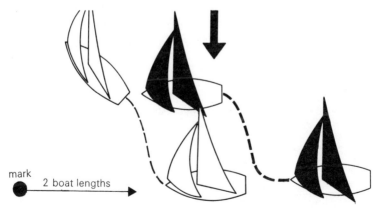

At this point he slows and bears away underneath White's stern, calls for water and slips neatly round the mark on the inside.

The following boat can also escape here by slowing down. She simply stops behind the leader, who cannot wait indefinitely in the two lengths' circle, and follows round the mark. The rules applying are discussed on page 126.

The Run

There is a lot to be said for being close behind on a run. It is the leg on which fortunes can change very swiftly, and there are several ways in which you can help to make them change in your favour. The wind shadow of one running boat is effective, but two close together can be devastating.

The turbulence here carries further ahead and extends over a much broader front than with a single rig. This greatly increased shadow can be used most usefully to affect a boat beyond the range of a single shadow or to delay a nearby boat more seriously.

Two teammates who decide to create such a wall to the wind should take care about how they position their boats. If they are too far apart the wind is actually accelerated through the gap (the venturi effect) and provides a stronger driving force for the boat ahead which is then helped on her way—exactly the opposite to what was intended.

Even round a single running rig there is some acceleration of the air flow round the mainsail, which shows on the flow diagram in Chapter 4 as closing up of the streamlines. It is therefore important when following to get the wind shadow exactly on the boat ahead. When there are two boats behind it matters even more because by getting into exactly the right place an opponent ahead can be very severely slowed down.

Setting up a wall of sail to prevent wind reaching the opposition was managed almost by accident once in the quarter finals of the Irish Dinghy Racing Association Team Racing Championships. London University had managed the starting beat very badly and rounded the weather mark 4, 5, 6. The wind was force 2 and the next leg was quite a short dead run. The position soon after the mark was—

London University

Dublin University

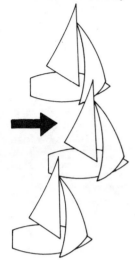

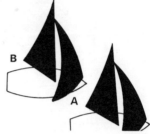

With the London boats presenting an impenetrable barrier to the wind, opposition B and C nearly stopped so that two London boats took inside berths and the position became

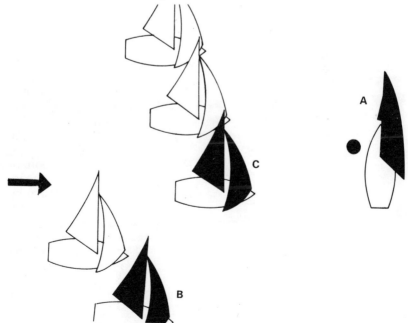

The fleet bunched up and even opponent A, in keeping clear by sailing wide and further, lost ground. London rounded with a leading 2, 3, 5 combination.

A run during the final of the 1970 Prince Philip Trophy shows both teams making good use of wind shadow. Team E, with darker jerseys lie 1st (out of the picture), 2nd and 5th.

118 (P) places windshadow on 480 (E), while 248 (P) is working up to put 483 (E) in wind shadow.

480 escapes 118's shadow and luffs towards 248. The mark ahead is to be left to starboard so 483 should luff 248 if she tries to take a windward overlap. If 248 manages to get close enough to make 483 luff, team P will benefit because 619 to leeward would come through into second place. Team P has to try to pass 483 and 480 to the back of the group if possible.

480 is making this more difficult for team P by working up to windward to draw 248's attention from the man ahead(483). If 480 threatens to take a windward overlap, 248 will have to luff, leaving 483 uncovered. E would then retain 1st and 2nd places.

Luffing on the run
Delaying an opponent by luffing is difficult on the run.

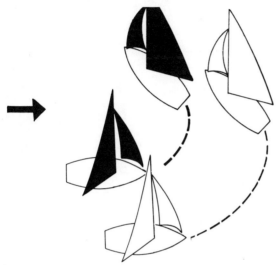

If Black's helmsman is not lined up to dive under White's transom as soon as the luff starts, then he can make a sharp luff himself which enables him to reach the mast abeam position well before head to wind. A prolonged luff works better:

next mark

White leads the way upwind without luffing too high. She sails in clear wind and can hold up Black to let a teammate pass.

It is possible to slow from astern by sitting very close to the leader's transom, dropping full centreplate and taking in the jib stick. The method works slowly and needs a long run before many boats lengths are lost. More ground can be lost by attacking to windward and inducing the man ahead to luff away from the direct line between marks.

The overlap at a leeward mark is so important that it is worth sacrificing a length to secure the inside berth. Losing ground to do so takes time when running before the wind and is best done by sweating the mainsail in hard, thereby presenting the least possible sail area to the wind. The manoeuvre works very well provided it is properly timed. It goes like this:

Black has caught White and established a leeward overlap, so White slows, sits on Black's wind and succeeds in gaining the vital overlap —just in time, and too late for Black to do the same to her. Black's only defence is to slow with White and prevent her dropping back: once White is close behind, Black is vulnerable. Having been forced outside, Black can now only hope to make a good rounding and take advantage of any weakness in White's turn.

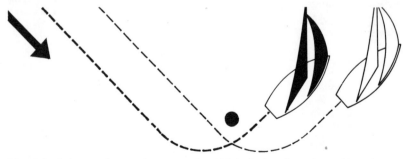

The black boat slows down under White's lee-bowing effect but at least she is in a position to tack immediately.

Starting Part 2

Although the start is, strictly speaking, the moment the start signal is made, the opening game is played for a minute or two before the gun and for a short time after. The period beforehand we shall look at in some detail, looking at general strategy and set plans. The first minute or so after the gun is a sorting out session from which the pattern of the first beat emerges; the time when the good starter climbs into first place and the poor one falls back to last. It is also a phase when boats are at close quarters and have ample opportunity to affect one another.

Windward starts

Teams which consistently demolish their opposition on the start line do so because each member has a distinct role to perform, each then knows what he is trying to do and, equally important, what his mates are up to. One goes for the ideal start in the bunch, a second makes a fast start clear of the rest, while a third is content to tie the opposition in knots and make the best of his start thereafter. Not only does this strategy leave the way open for at least two boats to make clear starts, but the fleet is reasonably spread and the opposition are denied a clear approach to the line.

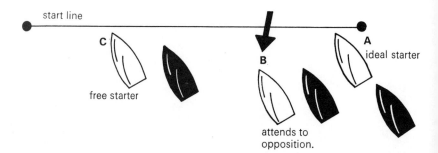

start line

C
free starter

B
attends to opposition.

A
ideal starter

White here makes exactly this sort of co-ordinated team start. Before going back to see how they got there, we shall first look at the working-out period that follows to see precisely why it is such a good combination.

Ideally White want C to take the lead and they contrive this through A and B pinching instead of sailing at top speed.

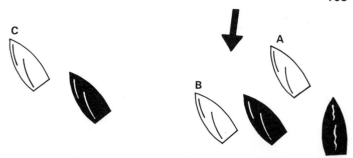

Already C, who started with a slight leeward disadvantage on the line, noses into the lead through the pinching policy of her mates. Black's tack cannot be ignored by A but she must hold on for a length or two to avoid tacking straight into a lee-bowed position. If A maintains her control of the starboard flank—as she is likely to do when the black boat tacks back—White dominate Black. White then goes on working in co-operation, defensively covering every move of Black's and at the same time attacking with wind shadow and lee-bow influence. The result is that the fleet will split into three pairs, with White controlling each pair.

Note particularly that A and B deliberately took the edge off their speed by pinching, on the one hand to let C clear and on the other to drive home their domination of the two nearby black boats.

The position could have been

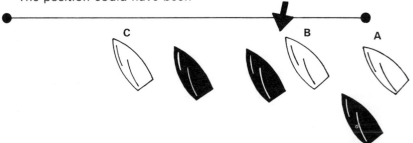

when A would still pinch but B would sail faster and freer than usual to ride over the boat to leeward and drop her into wind shadow. This facility to deviate a fraction high or low of the ideal windward course in order to drive home a tactical advantage is an extremely powerful ability, particularly during the first few minutes after the gun.

To go back to White's first start, the white boats have no real distance advantage over Black on the line yet their tactical position was good while Black's was bad. Why was White's start tactically superior? And how did they get into that position? The answers to these two questions tell a good deal about how to start as a team.

Control is the answer to the first question, each white boat has a high degree of control over her immediate opponent; by lee-bow against the two black boats near the line and wind shadow on the black boat further back.

But the control extends beyond adjacent pairs, as White's fleet is spread in a way which prevents any black boat breaking out of this tight position uncovered. Thus, while each opposition boat is taken care of, White is well placed to prevent any improvement which Black might try to make in their predicament.

To answer the second question—how White gained the better position—we can look at each helmsman's approach to the starting line bearing in mind his individual role. Boat A is the free starter and her helmsman makes the best individual start that he can, clear of the bunch, and in doing so lee-bows an opponent who is nearby. Making the best start of the fleet, A timed his run to hit the line on the gun right next to the mark; the following black boat was therefore unable to make the line on time as A was in the way. Meanwhile B had luffed smartly under the bow of an opponent and even if his own start suffered a little the black boat's suffered more.

The following sequence of pictures was taken at the start of the first race of the final of the Prince Philip Trophy in 1970 between Felixstowe Ferry (boats **a**, **b** and **c**) and London Corinthian. 10 seconds to go—

a, **b** and **c** are spread out and approaching the line at speed. 118 is a little early and is having to wait. 5 seconds to go—

483 is slowing down for fear of being over the line. **a** and **b** are still coming in at speed. The gun goes—

Boats **a**, **b** and **c** are reasonably spread along the line while their opposition are bunched further back. 5 seconds later—

c pinches to clear the starting mark but is in clear wind. So are **a** and **b**. Their opposition, meanwhile, are in difficulties. One boat is tacking, another is being lee-bowed, while the third is severely affected by dirty wind and is sailing low of a true windward course. But this was not the end of the race, for after being so strongly outstarted, Corinthian came back on the first beat and led by a narrow points margin round the first mark.

Starting from the reverse direction
The desirable close leeward position, which is the key to good team starting, is fairly easily gained by approaching the line from the reverse direction.

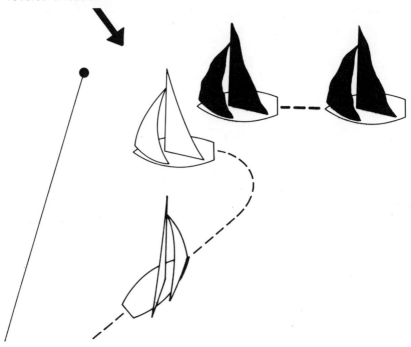

The oncoming black boat is a sitting target. The approach from the wrong side of the line is good for another reason too, the starting position is disclosed very late. Here it is obvious long before the gun goes where Black hopes to start. On the other hand White's position depends on which way she turns to come back to the line; if she tacks she will make a weather end start and if she gybes she will start to leeward.

A danger in a reverse run just before the start lies in an opponent doing the same directly astern. If the pursuer knows what he is doing he can prevent the first boat getting back to the line at all.

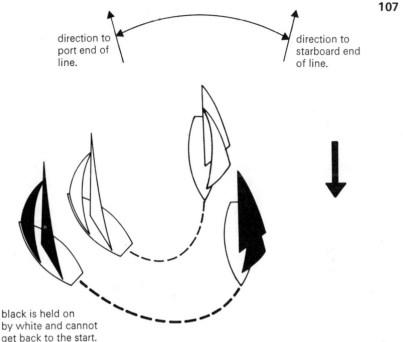

direction to port end of line.

direction to starboard end of line.

black is held on by white and cannot get back to the start.

Once into this position, White can hold Black away from the start line for as long as necessary. As soon as Black bears away to begin a gybe onto port, White has her nose in to leeward and Black cannot gybe without fouling White. If Black's helmsman now hardens up onto a beat, he is still unable to lay the line because White is in a position which prevents him from tacking. This ploy can be a good one for the following boat in some circumstances. If, for instance, she is the slowest of the fleet and cannot expect to do much better than sixth, then her helmsman is quite justified in driving a particularly strong opponent towards the lee shore. The technique is a familiar one to exponents of match racing and is widely used in the United States (where match racing is fairly popular) to outdo an opponent before the start.

Without actually driving him away from the start, a useful psychological move is to tail an opposing helmsman between the five-minute gun and the start, remaining within a boat's length the whole time. It is important when playing this sort of cat and mouse game to be the cat: if you tail someone attentively before the gun you do not want to be outstarted by him.

When there is a port bias to the line the roles of the team members remain similar but each man has to do his job rather differently. If the bias is slight and the fleet still tends to start towards the starboard end the free starter may try a port tack start—

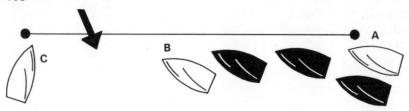

in which event B's task is to hold off both nearby black boats by pinching and slowing to allow C to cross clear ahead.

With more bias on the line and the fleet starting on port tack, the man whose job is to wreak what havoc he conveniently can among the opposition has a fine opportunity. He makes a point of starting on starboard and judges his approach to cross astern of his teammates.

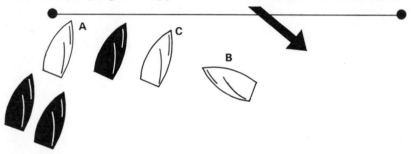

What happens when B, approaching at speed, meets the two port tack boats by the mark can well be imagined. Once more the start goes to White, and here again the role of each boat is clearly identified: B the spoiler, C the clear starter, A the pole position man. Not that this three way division is the only formula by which to split the responsibility, there are certainly others; but it is a method which has been used with consistent success by one or two top teams in recent years.

There is an interesting example of a start situation where the lee-bow position fails.

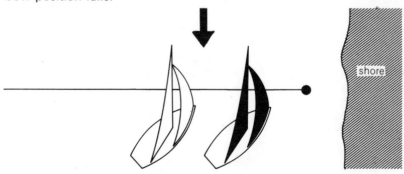

The port tack can only last a few lengths before Black calls water on White and their positions are reversed. On the starboard tack White takes command with a lee-bow, which just goes to show that you have to be wary of relying too much on hard and fast principles. Every problem you meet on the water has to be considered on its merits; situations are often similar but rarely identical.

A big bias in the line enables you to introduce a method of winning the start very decisively. Your three boats approach slowly in tight formation.

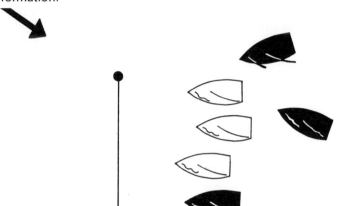

The weather boat makes an exact approach to the mark and the others take their line from her. The black boats are faced with a wall of hostile hulls, impenetrable because they are so close together and impassable to windward because of the distance mark. The leeward course past forces a boat taking it several lengths down straightaway. With Black thrown somewhat into confusion, White drives home the advantage after the gun by opening their ranks enough to allow each other clear wind: the weather boat pinches and leeward one powers off fractionally free.

Black can stop White building their wall before the start, and they do this by one of their men securing a good lee-bow berth on the windward white boat. If they gain a lee-bow on one other white boat—even the leeward one—Black are likely to win the start.

The biggest danger to White in making this type of start is that a black boat could luff the whole White team by luffing the leeward boat of the trio. The boat doing the luffing can approach from astern since the rules do not require you to be ahead of mast abeam when luffing before the start. This is therefore a risky start for White to try if their opponents are of the kind who are sharp on the rules and look for any opportunity to eliminate their opponents by collision and protest. If your opponents are of the collide-and-protest school, make a safer start and win by avoiding incidents and outsailing them.

In the moments before and after the start signal everything is in a state of flux; boats are in close combat and thinking has to be quick. In a team start the results are likely to be best when each man knows what he is trying to do and gets on with doing it. If only one of the three fails in his task the team is likely to start well; where all three do their part successfully the result is devastating. By any reckoning mistakes on the line are dear: half a length can make the difference between clear and dirty wind, the best and the worst start.

How Team Races are Run

Team races are organised some time in advance and their success depends on much more than good helmsmanship on the day. Selecting a suitable team to sail against, the type of boats used, the courses sailed, weather conditions, the start line and an efficiently manned race office all contribute to good racing.

Weather conditions
Although we cannot alter wind conditions, we can go some way to prevent extreme conditions of wind or calm from ruining the racing. For instance, survival conditions kill tactics, for then the aim is simply to get round the course if possible and as soon as possible. Violently flogging sails, upturned hulls and an almost uncontrollable boat to handle make life very exhilarating but they leave little time to think about the niceties of tactics. Yet conditions which are so extreme for

dinghies with full sail always seem less so when reefed (unless they have big genoas), and once you find the racing less of a hair-raising gymnastic experience you can begin to think more about the race and the other boats. As team racing's interest is largely in the tactics it introduces, reefing is sensible because it allows tactics to play a part in really heavy weather. The decision to reef is usually taken by the team captains if they are in agreement, or the race officer if they are not.

Very light airs make team racing unrewarding. The emphasis then is on keeping the boat moving and picking the best wind shifts; entangling with opposition boats is hazardous as almost anything can happen in such fickle conditions. In light and variable conditions it is far better to postpone the sailing a little and wait awhile if there is any prospect of a steady breeze.

Casual fixtures between clubs
One of the most pleasant ways in which to team race is against another club in an informal match. There is no need for the other club to sail the same type of boats as your own. The racing takes place on their water or yours in the home fleet—whatever class that happens to be. Competition between the classes, far from detracting from the racing, is an advantage and adds to the interest. You visit other people's sailing grounds, sail unfamiliar boats and different helmsmen race in your own boats.

This variety, together with the pleasant social side of most interclub matches, has helped to make team racing as popular as it is in Britain today.

The host club provides six boats for the match and at least one spare in case of gear failure; the visitors need only arrive with their waterproof clothes and sailing skill. As no one trails any boats around, matches can be arranged between clubs quite far apart; this considerably widens the scope for selecting clubs to sail against. Because the two races required to decide a match take no more than half a day to sail, including putting the boats in the water and taking them out, fixtures are easily arranged so as not to interfere with normal club racing. In any case, there is nothing to prevent a match being sailed at the same time as the home club's points series.

If two clubs which are already fairly good at team racing want to improve their standard, it is not a bad idea to select teams consisting of one pundit helmsman and two less experienced. The teams are then still well matched and the less experienced have a chance to be guided by their captain and see real team racing—difficult usually, unless they crew regularly.

Matching
Poor team races are often predictable before the start signal goes; teams may be badly matched, with one clearly more expert than the other. Pairing teams of about equal standard is straightforward when all the helmsmen sail in the same class, since open meetings give some idea of helming ability. It is more difficult when they sail different classes. Nevertheless, some effort to select matches with clubs of about equal strength is worthwhile; the racing is likely to be much closer and more exciting as a result.

Leagues as we know them in football and cricket are a recent innovation in team racing. The first began among a number of northern universities. The second was formed in 1970 among twelve leading team racing clubs in the south of England, by Dr John

Barker and the author. Although no formal leagues existed until recently, the benefit of good matching has been appreciated for some time, and universities frequently sail a second team against weaker opposition. Matching is an important facet of the racing since runaway victories are devoid of any tactics and are tedious, whereas good team racing—at any level—usually occurs when sides of near equal standard meet.

Courses
Ideally courses should be fairly short with short legs. Since windward work and dead runs provide the most opportunities for overtaking and teamwork, the race tends to be more interesting when centred around them. Reaches, as earlier chapters showed, depend more than other points of sailing on sheer boat speed, and tactics are restricted. Reaching should be limited, but not too severely, as the essence of a good course is variety—a constantly changing pattern to the race and new problems, the prospect of another leg with fresh chances for overtaking. For this reason several rounds of a small course are better than a single longer round which gives the same race duration.

Start lines
The best start lines are short. The fleet is then thrown together straight away. Lines are easily set since there is not the same need for a true windward start as with individual competition. In practice, even downwind starts work fairly well. They encourage a bunch at the first mark admittedly, but this makes the beginning of the beat which follows close and interesting. Start lines can be varied: a true windward line as often as possible but occasionally a reach or even a run.

The line has to be clearly defined so that when on the water competitors know precisely where it is. When short transits are used distance marks are useless if they are behind the line, for boats can legitimately start outside them. Distance mark buoys have to be on or over the line.

Suitable boats
Team competitions can take place successfully within any racing class where the speed of individual boats is fairly similar, from little Optimists to Dragons. But the best team racing is in one-design dinghies between twelve and fifteen feet long. These boats are not out-and-out helmsman tailored, high performance craft and individual boat speed tends to be fairly consistent. To eliminate the difference in boat performance completely and make the contest one of helming skill only, teams swap boats between races.

The specialised two-man, trapeze dinghies like Flying Dutchmen are too individual in performance and fitting layout to be good team race boats: it is impractical for helmsmen to swap boats between races and the finer points of tactics are lost to sheer speed through the water. This does not make team racing impossible in these highly tuned classes but it does reduce the importance of tactics.

505s racing for the Ale Yard Trophy at Pitsford—an annual event in which about 25 four-boat teams compete.

Fireflys, 420's, GP 14's and similar craft in which competitive fleets tend to stay fairly close together provide excellent team racing, and most team competition is in such classes. The Wilson Trophy, for which 32 teams compete, is sailed in Fireflys. The final rounds of the RYA National Team competition have been in Larks, Fireflys, Enterprises and GP 14's.

One-design keel boats can give good team racing, but cannot provide the quick action which is to be found in the best dinghy contests.

Spinnakers A spinnaker makes racing more a matter of speed and less a problem of tactics. Quickly set and properly handled it can wipe out all the ground lost on the beat in a few seconds. It is also rather a personal sail in that fittings and sheeting arrangements vary enormously, so boat swapping becomes difficult.

The short legs of a team race course make the spinnaker, in any but the most expert hands, an awkward sail to handle. In most matches, therefore, spinnakers are not used, and the RYA National Team Racing Championship discourages their use. The sail is hardly missed for there is usually enough to think about otherwise.

The number of boats
Teams are best made up of three boats. Two is pointless with the normal scoring system as the race is solely for first place—anything that happens behind is irrelevant. The most sensible way to race two

boat teams is to lay down that the side with last boat home loses and this arrangement gives perfectly good racing. Four boats a side in any but the most experienced hands tend to make racing more a battle between boats than teams. Good team competition can be found in four boat matches: matches in International 14's between Britain, America, Canada and Bermuda are sailed with four boats, so too are matches between the British Universities and the Combined Services in Fireflys. On the sea and with longer courses some of the most experienced helmsmen prefer four and even five boat teams, but on inland waters and on the short courses recommended in this book three is the best number and the vast majority of team racing takes place with three boat teams.

Knockout competitions

Competitions arranged on a knockout basis for a large number of teams and sailed throughout a weekend have become very popular.

The first of these team meetings was the Irish Dinghy Racing Championship held at Dun Laoghaire near Dublin. The second was the Wilson Trophy, first sailed in 1948 and held at West Kirby in Cheshire. These set a pattern which others have followed.

Entry to the Wilson Trophy is limited to 32 teams since that is the maximum number the host club can cope with in one weekend. Teams come from all over Britain and Eire to sail in the event, which is a straightforward knockout competition. Each match in the competition is decided on points aggregate over two races and boats are swapped between each.

West Kirby Sailing Club provide the boats, which they arrange into fleets of threes. Each fleet is identified by coloured racing flags. The race officer has to start and finish 63 matches (126 races) in two days to complete the programme, which requires a highly organised shore staff as well as a supply of spare boats, rescue facilities, food and refreshments. The whole operation is planned months ahead each year and works to a tight schedule. The races are short and the sailing water is a small marine lake, which provides excellent close racing.

Several other meetings extend to only 16 teams and the manpower and organisation necessary for this size of competition is far less than for 32. The job of organising is considerably eased if helmsmen bring their own boats, though the competition falls short of the ideal as there is no swapping to cancel boat speed differences. But it does work and several competitions are arranged in this way, not only for the smaller dinghies but for 505's and Fireballs.

Two day league competitions

The sudden death of a knockout competition is unfortunate for a team that has travelled a long way to sail. A form of weekend American

Tournament has therefore been developed which gives a more even spread of races to winners and losers. Crews bring their own boats. The entries are split equally into four groups and in each group a league is held where each team sails one race against every other team in the group. Four teams eventually emerge as finalists, one from each section. They then sail one race against each other—three races in all. The winner is decided by counting the wins or, if a tie has to be broken, by adding the total points.

Where one race only is sailed against other teams, wins rather than points must be the first decider, otherwise it is possible to end up with a winning team which has lost one race and a runner-up which has lost none. This happens when one team beats the other three by small margins while one of the beaten sides gains big wins in its other two races. The undefeated team should always be the victor regardless of points. The winner is more convincingly decided if the two top teams of the final four sail a second race together. They will already have sailed against each other once in the final so that the second (and last) race uses the earlier one as its first leg. In other words their deciding match has two races and the points for both are added to give the winner. Alternatively, a straight knockout contest with a semi-final and final among these last four teams works well.

The race officer

The race officer has an unenviable job to do at the best of times. He is there solely for the benefit of the racing fleet. He is its servant but at the same time, if he is to do his job properly, its master. His aim should always be to provide the best racing that conditions will allow: i.e. good courses, good start lines, and efficient starting and finishing procedures.

The starts, finishes and courses have already been dealt with. They are, however, the responsibility of the race officer, though if he is wise he will take notice of the team captains' opinions about course setting. There are special requirements for a team race course, a fact that race officers unfamiliar with team racing do not always realise. Courses of the right length are best set before the race rather than using the shortening procedure which works so well for individual racing. In team racing it is less satisfactory, as shortening might reverse the result of a close contest.

Premature starters should be recalled as soon as possible; neglecting to do this spoils the match because the points penalty for disqualification is so severe. The late recall of a premature starter often condemns him to last place, but this is less crippling than disqualification. Jumping the gun is, of course, the fault of the helmsman responsible, but a good race officer lets the offender know straightaway.

Applying the rules

At ordinary open meetings protests can be settled by a committee made up of experienced sailors who are not competing. This ensures that a competent, unbiased committee is always at hand and racing is not held up unnecessarily. The difficulty lies in finding volunteers, but for the RYA Team Trophy, the British Universities Championships and one or two other important meetings an independent protest committee always stands by. In smaller competitions this is unnecessary, although it is characteristic of keen team racing that the sailing throws up protests more often than individual competition.

In casual fixtures between clubs, settling protests can be a problem, since finding a committee which is both independent and competent is sometimes impossible. Often one member of each side who is not directly involved in the disputed incident and an outsider to chair the meeting can resolve the incident perfectly well. Members of the home club selected for their independence rather than for what they know about the rules make poor committees—and sometimes remarkable decisions.

In hearing protests against the race officer no one associated with the race management on that day may sit on the committee.

Gear failure

A strange heading in a chapter on race management perhaps, but unfortunately gear failure is a common enough phenomenon to warrant it. When the racing is in a pool of six boats swapped between races, gear failure which is not the fault of the crew means that the race must be resailed. Fair as this rule is, some exciting and keenly fought matches have been spoiled by failures of this sort. The answer is to have well equipped boats which are unlikely to break

down. When helmsmen do not swap, but sail their own boats throughout, gear failure is their own responsibility, so resails are not usually
allowed on this count.

RYA Team Championships

Team racing had become so popular in Britain by the end of the 60's
that in 1969 the RYA organised the first National Team Championship. Two hundred and sixty teams entered from all over the country,
and even from outside Britain—several teams entered from Southern
Ireland, where team racing has been popular for some time. The
entries were divided into 12 areas, and in each area a knockout
competition was held.

Each match of this knockout was held on the home waters of one
of the two clubs and sailed in the home team's boats. The visitors had
a choice of boats, but if they wanted the racing to be in any other
than those offered they had to bring six boats themselves. The semi-
finals and finals in each area were sailed on neutral water. Spinnakers
were not allowed in the competition and crews changed boats
between races. The winner was decided as a result of one weekend's
racing among the twelve finalists: two elimination leagues of six
teams culminated in a knockout competition between four, the top
two from each league. A trophy was presented by Prince Philip.

The first competition was won by West Kirby, the second, in which
there were 350 entries, by Felixstowe Ferry. West Kirby followed their
victory by winning the first European competition to be held, which
included top club teams from France, Holland, Germany and Belgium.

The finalists vie for a lead in the RYA final of 1970, 2nd race

In Universities

Fourteen teams sailed in the first British Universities Championship. That was in 1957, in 1969 36 teams entered. In 1939 only two universities, Oxford and Cambridge, team raced; in 1969 the number was 50.

The reasons for this impressive increase in university clubs which team race are interesting. Most university sailing clubs can afford only a small number of boats, too few for exciting individual competition but enough for team racing. Matches between universities became possible and a full scale National Championship encouraged competition. Undergraduate examinations are in the summer so the best time for their sailing is in winter, and as team races are short and concentrated, they are ideal for frostbite racing. These are the contributing factors, but the significance of the growth is undeniably that, however convenient and suitable the racing, students enjoy team racing more than individual racing. London University first team, for instance, sails more than twenty five matches a year which, together with about half that number each for the second and ladies' teams, amounts to a lot of racing for one club in a year.

International matches between European universities have frequently taken place since the first, between Britain and France in Paris in 1959. A European Universities Championship is now regularly held. Not that international student sailing is confined to Europe, for in 1965 the British Universities sailed against the American Universities at London in a fixture which has since become a bi-annual event.

Internationally

The British-American Cup series in Six Metres, followed by the International 14 series made team racing an international sport from the start. But whereas the increase in the popularity of team racing in Britain and Ireland has been considerable, few other countries have seriously taken it up. (A notable exception is Madagascar, where twenty seven clubs team race, and who proposed team racing as a sport to be included in the Olympic Games). Some team racing goes on in North America, but match racing is their main variant to normal club racing. In Europe, outside Britain and Ireland, interest is small but increasing.

What Next?

More people team race each year. Interest abroad is increasing, and a European Championship is now an annual event. Team racing was rejected when suggested as an Olympic sport in 1967: that was perhaps less surprising than that anyone put it forward at all at this stage in its development. The sport has been suggested more seriously for the Commonwealth Games.

Before international acceptance comes the ordinary rules of racing will have to be better known and enforced. Given the spur of national prestige, matches could become very acrimonious and already, experience in university matches at home and abroad bears this out.

For team racing to become more widespread there must first be interest and then some sort of overall organisation. Nationally, the RYA team competition owes its success to both. If sufficient interest were to develop abroad, in a few years time a World Championship would be worth organising. It would not be a particularly difficult task.

As a distinct and parallel development of team racing as we now know it, there is no reason why a radically different approach to team sailing could not produce a quite new type of competition. Why not invent an entirely new game in boats which breaks away completely from traditional racing? A scheme which reached the trial stage is worth mentioning.

One boat only on each side sails the course, and the first one home wins the match for her team. Just like match racing so far, but here is the difference: three boats on each side hover around the two key boats, and these satellite sailors are not required to sail the course. They are permitted to cut corners as they please, and have no rights over the two key boats, but in every other way are bound by the IYRU rules. What happens in practice is that one satellite concentrates on hindering the opposition key boat with dirty wind while the other two satellites try to clear a way for her through the opposition ranks.

That is one possible alternative to team racing and there are certainly others. Perhaps we shall not always pursue each other round fixed buoys to win our sailing competitions. The idea is hard to take, but so, thirty years ago, was the idea that you could win any sort of satisfactory sailing contest by sailing slowly on occasion—but it's true.

The Rules and their Interpretation

The rules are more terrifying and rather less exhilarating to many yachtsmen than a whole gale of wind. Although we can hardly make them as exciting as the sailing itself, it is perhaps possible to illuminate some of the darker corners of a subject that all sailors can know more about. The subject is a big one and there is no need for a helmsman to know case history and all the rest of it, but he does need to know what the rules lay down about the most common events that occur on the water. If he does not he will be like the man at a dinner party who is scared to take a first mouthful for fear of using the wrong fork. To be diffident and give way on the water through lack of rule knowledge is definitely not the way to win races.

Controversial events in team racing are often very different from those in individual competition. Besides the whole repertoire of incidents of individual contests there are others, and these incidents special to team racing are the ones that are dealt with here, the most common of them anyway. In team racing a helmsmen frequently seeks out a battle with an opponent, usually to slow him down, and this makes the game essentially more aggressive than any other form of sailing. Courses and starts are designed to keep the fleet somewhat bunched and there are more marks to round, which makes the rules matter more too. Not that this is any reason for anyone to be put off team racing, on the contrary there is probably no quicker way to learn about tactics and rules: everyone on both sides is directly interested in infringements of the rules, whether they actually caused them or not, for the result of the match often depends on the outcome. Many people find this an easy way to learn what the rules actually mean, and how they work on the water.

Reaching
A leading boat intent on slowing another on a reach may not sail below her proper course to prevent the victim overtaking to leeward when the boats are within three boat lengths of one another.

Rule 39 applies
'A yacht which is on a free leg of the course shall not sail below her *proper course* when she is clearly within three of her overall lengths of either a *leeward yacht* or a yacht *clear astern* which is steering a course to pass to *leeward*.'

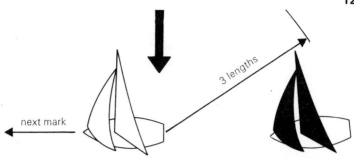

The leader here has to sail in the fastest direction to the next mark, which is usually a straight line towards it.

Notice that the yacht astern must be 'steering a course to pass to leeward'. If she is following directly astern on the same course as the leader or is upwind sailing in the same direction then the leader is perfectly entitled to steer below a proper course. To gain the protection of Rule 39 the yacht astern must aim to leeward of the other before hailing and be within three boat lengths. It is usual and courteous to hail a yacht contravening Rule 39 and only protest if she persists after the warning.

The same rule prevents a yacht which is finishing on a free leg of the course from choosing whichever end she pleases of the finishing line. The definition of proper course includes the phrase 'to finish as quickly as possible', which leaves no room for doubt about which end of the finishing line a yacht bound by Rule 39 must go for: the nearest (except occasionally in special conditions of tide or wind where the furthest end would be favourable).

Luffing a boat the wrong side of a mark
A yacht luffing another the wrong side of a mark may also find herself on the wrong side of the law if her helmsman is not conversant with the rule that applies specifically to the manoeuvre: 42.1 (a) (iv). It refers to two yachts about to round a mark on the required side. 'An outside leeward yacht with luffing rights may take an inside yacht to windward of a mark provided that she hails to that effect and begins to luff before she is within two of her overall lengths of the mark and provided that she also passes to windward of it.'

So the procedure for the boat ahead with luffing rights that decides to carry out this manoeuvre is (a) hail before her bow is within two lengths of the mark (b) luff the other boat upwind of the mark (c) sail upwind of the mark herself before returning to sail round the right way. A boat passes to windward of a mark when she leaves the mark to leeward (that is, on the same side as her boom) and passes an imaginary line drawn through the mark at right angles to the direction of the previous mark.

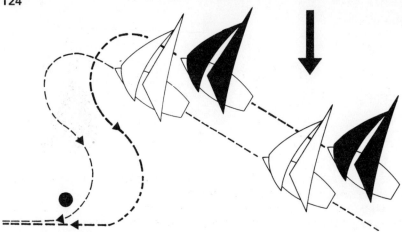

Once the white boat has sailed past a line drawn through the mark at right angles to the direction of the previous mark, she has fulfilled her obligation to pass to windward of the mark.

Manoeuvring against the last boat on the final leg

Rule 2 of the Team Racing Rules drawn up in the Appendix of the IYRU Yacht Racing Rules says, 'Except to protect her own or a team-mate's finishing position, a yacht in one team which is completing the last leg of the course shall not manoeuvre against a yacht in another team which has no opponent astern of her.' This prevents boats of one team dropping back to harass an opposition boat lying last with the sole intention of forcing her to retire.

Rounding a mark

Team Racing Rule 4 makes it quite clear what a boat is entitled to do with another which lies outside her as both approach a mark to make a rounding. The rule adds nothing that is not already in the main body of the rule book, merely reinforces. The luff here is perfectly legitimate and no hail is necessary:

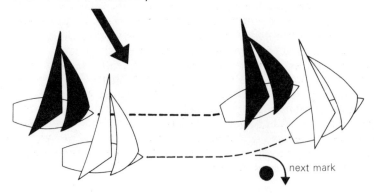

next mark

But this is not allowed :

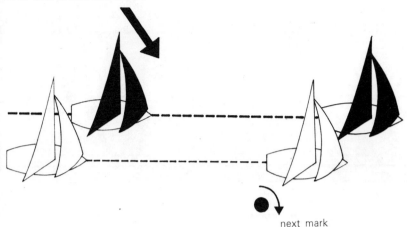

next mark

Because White has no luffing rights and is the inside yacht she is bound by Team Racing Rule 4 (a) and also by Rule 42.1(a)(ii). She must gybe at the first reasonable opportunity.

Rule 4 (b) allows something permitted in individual racing, but which no one in their right mind would ever do.

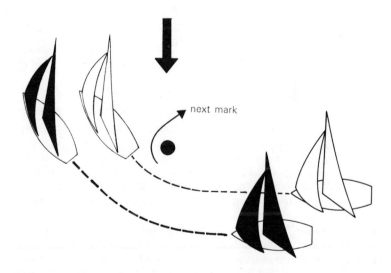

next mark

The windward boat is not obliged to tack but need only sail as high as closehauled unless luffed by the leeward yacht.

But the following is not a permissible move by White—

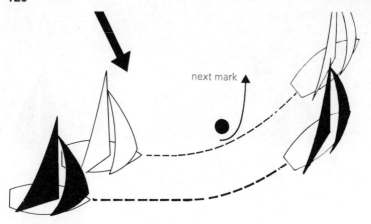

The white boat here may not sail below her proper course after the rounding.

Two lengths trap

One manoeuvre, which entered the repertoire of team tactics six years ago in the final of the British Universities Championship, is to hover stationary within the two lengths' circle.

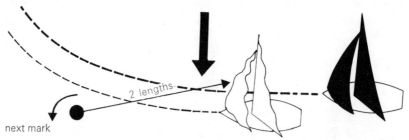

When the helmsman of the black boat approaches he has a problem. If he goes to leeward he is barging, so that if the white boat hits him while bearing away to round the mark, Black is out. On the other hand an attempt to pass to windward invites a strong luff. It is a desperate manoeuvre but it can work and is perfectly legitimate so long as: (1) the leading boat has luffing rights, (2) her bow is inside the two lengths' circle and (3) she is the inside boat if they overlap before reaching the two lengths' circle.

Luffing the wrong side of a mark 42.1 (a) (iv) does not apply for it requires the leeward yacht to be outside at the mark. The leeward yacht above is inside. The black boat above could not legitimately have attempted to pass to leeward of White claiming water at the mark, for as long as the white boat's bow is within two lengths of the mark White is entitled to the inside berth herself.

Manoeuvring against a yacht on another leg of the course
To prevent a boat on one leg of the course deliberately sailing out of her way to interfere with a boat on another leg of the course Team Racing Rule 1 lays down, 'A yacht may manoeuvre against a yacht sailing on another leg of the course only if she can do so while sailing a proper course relative to the leg on which she herself is sailing.' The rule prevents undesirable surprise tactics; for instance on a windward leg it prevents a boat running through the tacking fleet from deliberately sailing off course to create havoc among the opposition. It also prevents a boat in last place from cutting corners to alter the race positions up front and then dropping back into her last place with nothing other than distance lost.

A question put to the RYA concerned the definition of the same leg of the course. Difficulty arose when sailing on a course of several rounds and one boat capsized. The helmsman righted her only to find that his side was now losing. Meanwhile the fleet had almost caught him up again, so he slowed the leader of the race—who was on the other side—to the back of the bunch, thereby reversing the result. The question arises, was he sailing on the same leg of the course as a race leader exactly one lap ahead?

The RYA decided a few years ago that he was on the same leg of the course, and that is the interpretation published in the earlier printings of this book. They have since changed their minds : the two boats are not now regarded as being on the same leg of the course, so waiting a lap and slowing the leader is not allowed.

Sailing away from the starting line
There is no proper course before the starting signal so it is quite in order to tail another boat and deliberately sail her away from the starting line, either by broad reaching behind her or holding her on one tack closehauled. (The means of doing this are described on page 107.)

Collisions
The rule book says 'A right of way yacht which fails to make a reasonable attempt to avoid a collision resulting in serious damage may be disqualified as well as the other yacht.' (Rule 32). In borrowed boats avoidance of collisions, so far as that is possible, is even more important than when helmsmen are sailing their own. Serious, in this context, is taken as meaning sufficiently crippling to incapacitate her. Holes in the side which let water in when sailing, or failure of a shroud due to a collision are typical examples of serious damage.

At a team meeting a local rule written into the sailing instructions to discourage irresponsibility in borrowed boats is no bad thing, so long as its application is consistent.

On collisions between teammates the IYRU have reversed an

earlier decision and decided that these would not be penalised and, under Rule 3 of the team racing appendix, one of the two teammates must retire after a collision between them. If neither retires immediately the poorer-scoring teammate will automatically be disqualified.

Waiving right of way to a teammate
Rights may be waived among teammates so long as an opponent is not baulked (Team Racing Rule 3). Which means that if someone on the other side has to take avoiding action as a direct result of teammates waiving rights then one of the teammates is in the wrong.

Team Racing Rule 3 goes on to say that if a collision between two teammates results in damage serious enough to disable either boat, the race committee is not entitled to cancel or abandon the race under Rule 12 (yacht materially prejudiced).

Windward work—sailing below a proper course
A yacht sailing to windward may sail below her proper course to position herself on the wind of a boat on the same tack—provided she does not cause the leeward yacht to alter course to avoid her.

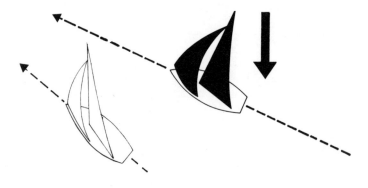

This is therefore a perfectly legitimate course for Black so long as the white boat does not have to keep out of her way. Notice that we are talking about windward work only here, the position is quite different downwind. Rule 39 (sailing below a proper course) applies to a free leg of the course, but not to the beat.

A yacht is entitled deliberately to hold another on to overstand a mark, because nowhere in the rules book is there any obligation to tack except to clear an obstruction to sea room. The yacht forcing the other to overstand can be either clear astern or overlapped, it makes no difference. The only limitations are obstructions to sea room which would entitle the yacht which was prevented from tacking—the one held on—to call for water. She has, incidentally, the right to choose which side she passes an obstruction; whether she heads up, bears away round it or tacks to clear is entirely up to her helmsman. Though an excursion round an obstruction by the longest route might, in the extreme, be a case of sailing below a proper course.

Braking

Braking devices or any other method to 'check way by abnormal means' are forbidden by Rule 60. Not that any dinghy classes are fitted with brakes, but there are less obvious forbidden braking methods like putting a foot or a bailing bucket over the side. A helmsman who heels the boat to windward and then, deliberately to slow the boat, drapes himself so far over the side that his backside drops into the water also acts illegally. Colliding with a teammate to check way is also an abnormal means of slowing, yet letting the sheets fly or even backing the jib to stop is not.

This brings us to the legality of slowing down in close proximity to other boats to gain a tactical advantage.

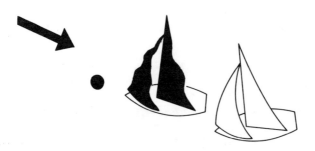

The leader here slows to force the second boat outside; once she is outside the leader has water at the mark and can tack. Is slowing in this example, where a nearby boat has to take avoiding action, legal? The answer is yes, there is nothing in the rules to prevent it—provided the leader does not alter course in the process. Alteration of course is prohibited by Rule 34—Limitations on the right-of-way yacht to alter course. The rule is about altering course, not increasing or reducing speed. This means that the manoeuvres on pages 68 and 69 are quite legitimate.

Questions to the RYA

It is in the nature of team racing to produce more contentious incidents than other forms of sailing, and the resulting protests are not always easy to decide. Sometimes incidents are sufficiently unusual for three to be no case history on the point in question, so no protest committee in one of these cases could be confident about its decision. An appeal to the RYA is the traditional method of resolution, but there is another which is well worth adopting. The RYA answer questions on points of law and these questions go through the Racing Rules Committee—a particularly useful service to protest committees since a protestor who loses is not always interested in appealing.

The following set of questions, and the RYA's answers, which are reproduced in full, show how helpful it can be to ask when you do not know the answer. The questions were posed by the University of London SC and the British Universities Sailing Association.

1965 I.Y.R.U. racing rules
CASE 9
University of London Sailing Club
British Universities Sailing Association
Definitions of Luffing and Proper Course and rules 34, 37.1, 38.1, 41.4 and 49.—*Unfair team racing tactics. Heeling or rolling a yacht to cause contact and simultaneous tacking.*

Questions:

In team racing, difficult problems arise concerning the interpretation of the racing rules. Two of the manoeuvres queried below involve contact between yachts with the sole object of 'putting out' an opponent. It will be apparent from the examples given, that some unfortunate tendencies are becoming prevalent in university team racing. We should be grateful for a clarification of the extent to which the specific sanction of rule 49 may be applied as a weapon against them.

Question

Situation A, Definition of Proper Course.

Proper Course is defined in terms of a yacht's 'course'.

Does this mean the direction along her centre line (i.e., the direction in which she is pointing) or the direction of her actual course made good through the water?

It is possible to alter the course made good in a number of ways without altering the direction in which the yacht is pointing,

 e.g. (i) by sailing with the centreboard raised, or

    (ii) by abnormal trimming of the mainsail, so that her principal movement is leeway.

Answer

Situation A.

 The definition of 'Proper Course' refers to the course made good through the water and not to the direction in which the yacht is pointing. Royal North of Ireland Yacht Club, Y.R.A., 1937/6, refers.

Question

Situation B, Rule 38.1—Right-of-Way Yacht Luffing after Starting.

     Rule 34—Misleading or Baulking,

     Rule 49—Fair Sailing.

1. Two yachts in opposing teams are close-hauled on the same tack. The leeward yacht has luffing rights and, without altering course, heels to windward so that her masthead touches the mast or sail of the windward yacht.

  If it can be established that this heeling to windward was deliberate (e.g., by both crew members of a dinghy sitting to windward in light winds):-

 (a) does this manoeuvre constitute a luff;

 (b) can rule 34 or rule 49 apply; and

 (c) is this manoeuvre legal?

2. What is the situation if it cannot be established that this manoeuvre was deliberate?

3. What is the situation if the leeward yacht has no luffing rights?

4. If two or more yachts in the same team deliberately heel to windward at the time of the starting signal, thereby occupying a large part of a short starting line, does this constitute unfair sailing under rule 49? In this particular case a masthead collision occurred between two yachts in opposing teams.

Answer

Situation B.

1. (a) No, because by definition, luffing involves altering course.

  (b) Rule 34 cannot apply because it requires the right-of-way yacht '...not...so to *alter course*...' as to prevent the other yacht from keeping clear or mislead or baulk her while she is keeping clear.

  (c) No. If carried out deliberately and with the sole intention of disqualifying the windward yacht, it contravenes rule 49.

2. The situation would be governed by rule 37.1.

3. As the leeward yacht did not alter course, whether or not she had luffing rights is irrelevant.

4. Deliberately to heel a yacht to windward, without altering course, with the sole object of either touching a windward yacht or forcing her to keep clear, is, in the opinion of the appeals com-

mittee, a clear-cut violation of the principles laid down in rule 49 and, as no other rule applies, a race committee is entitled to act under it against such a yacht.

Question

Situation C, Rule 41.4—Tacking at the Same Time,
Rule 34—Misleading or Baulking,
Rule 49—Fair Sailing.

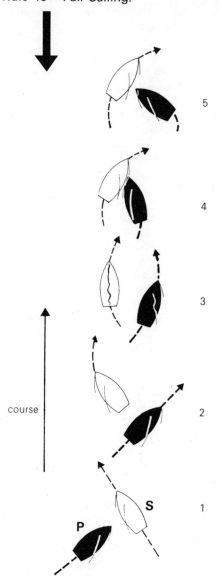

On a beat, a starboard-tack dinghy, *S*, crosses ahead of a port-tack dinghy, *P*, in the opposing team (position 1) and starts to luff preparatory to tacking into a covering position on *P*'s bow (position 2).

P's helmsman, seeing *S* luffing, quickly puts his helm down, starting a fast tack on to *S's* starboard quarter, in such a way that *P's* bow hits *S's* quarter before *S* can complete her tack (positions 3, 4 and 5).

This whole manoeuvre is so rapid that *S* has insufficient time either to resume her original starboard tack or to complete her new port tack—i.e., it is impossible for her to keep clear.

It is very hard to establish that this manoeuvre is deliberate. If it can be shown to be deliberate:-

(i) Does rule 34 or rule 49 apply?

(ii) Is this manoeuvre legal?

Answer

Situation C.

Rule 34 applies.

P began to tack after she was aware that *S* was tacking.

Therefore, as the yachts did not begin to tack at the same time, rule 41.4 did not apply.

While tacking, *S* was bound by rule 41.1 to keep clear of *P*, the yacht on a tack. The diagrams indicate that *S* would have complied with this obligation if *P* had held her course. By tacking when she did, *P* infringed rule 34.1 (a) which, being in Section A of Part IV, always applies and, in the circumstances, over-rides rule 41.1.

Making the rules work

It is one thing to lay down rules and another to enforce them. Sailing is about the only athletic game in which there is no umpire. We settle disputes among ourselves and in many ways this is an excellent arrangement, but it is open to abuse. G. Sambrook Sturgess, Chairman of the IYRU Rules Committee, says in his book Yacht Racing, on the subject of the fair sailing rule 'It presupposes that competitors are men of goodwill, of complete integrity and of undoubted veracity.' He might just as well have been talking about the whole rule system, for unless people tell the truth in protest meetings the system fails and we need umpires.

Independent witnesses are always valuable to protest committees, but as everyone in a team race is an interested party independent witnesses are hard to come by. In most casual inter-club matches this does not matter and the system works perfectly well as it stands. Unfortunately, when the stakes are high enough, when people want to win really badly some of them lie in protest meetings; and often they do win—really badly. Only very few people who team race give false evidence admittedly, but it happens often enough to warrant, in the most important competitions, some sort of protection to those who tell the truth in front of a protest meeting.

Often, an incident in dispute depends on the onus of proof : a port tacker, for instance, who claims that a starboard boat headed up violently to touch his rudder has to prove that the starboard tacker did actually head up sharply. If the starboard tack helmsman is of the kind that tries such a manoeuvre to disqualify an opponent, he may well deny his alteration of course when it comes to the protest meeting. The onus is then on the port tacker to prove the other man's luff in order to win the decision. But unfortunately without a witness, preferably unbiased, the port tacker has little chance of winning— even though he was deliberately fouled.

The problem is not unique to team racing. Given high enough stakes in individual competition—an Olympic medal for instance— it is sometimes not certain whether the two parties are even talking about the same incident. In the Olympic Games an answer has been found to this enforcement problem. At Tokyo in 1964 each racing fleet was followed by observer launches with photographers on board. The photographers were guided by experienced sailors who told them what to shoot. The result was that the protest committee had a photographic record of each incident, which was covered by perhaps as many as twenty consecutive pictures. In themselves the pictures were not always conclusive but nevertheless they were extremely useful in deciding which of two conflicting stories was nearer the truth. Contestants became more wary of protesting and exaggerated claims about what actually happened were rarer.

A system which is similar in principle but easier to operate has been used in the RYA National Team Racing finals. Instead of using inflatable marks, the course is laid by mooring small rowing boats as marks and from these mark boats observers watch the fleet. This means that for incidents which happen at marks—and in top-level team racing that's where most of them do happen—there is an independent expert observer to tell the protest committee who he thought hit what where and when. This system works well enough for it to have been used every year at the team finals since its intro-duction in 1971, and provided the protest committee doesn't consider the evidence of observers to be infallible (they have a lot to watch out for and remember) the competition is certainly fairer.

Alternative Penalties

Team racing has been criticised for breeding a particularly nasty kind of sailor who deliberately goes out of his way to put out one of the boats he is sailing against. Regardless of all the moralising about sportsmanship, fair play and so on, it was at one time almost common practice to try to win in the protest room a match that was lost on the water. Rather than try to change the attitudes of helmsman by moralising, I suggested, when this book first appeared, an alternative scoring system for team races designed to discourage protests and leave race-winning to sailors, not protesters. In the intervening three years Castaways have pioneered the system so that with minor changes it has been used more and more until last year it replaced the traditional scoring system in the area and national finals of the RYA competition.

The big problem with the traditional points system is that retirement in a team race is disastrous for the side which loses the boat. It's a double penalty : two boats are left with the impossible task of trying to handle three opponents and the boat that drops out takes 7 points instead of her finishing score—at worst, 6 points. What's more, the penalty is unequal. A helmsman who is likely to finish in first place suffers a $6\frac{1}{4}$ point loss (7 minus $\frac{3}{4}$) while a man who was heading for last place anyway is only 1 point worse off (7 minus 6), although the offences may have been identical.

This means that if your opponents can put out your best man before the start the match would be all over bar the shouting, of which there'd be a lot.

Too much at the moment therefore hinges on rule infringements, so the new system reduces the size of the penalty and leaves everyone racing—which means that three boats are always sailing against three. The penalty for infringing a rule and acknowledging the infringement is 2 points and is added to the finishing score. When the infringement is not acknowledged and has to go to protest, the points penalty is 4. No one drops out ; they simply sail on after infringing and either acknowledge their mistake by tying a green flag to the shroud, or dispute it by flying a red flag.

If the boat that disputes an incident finishes first and loses the protest, she will receive $\frac{3}{4}+4$ points. Had she conceded the infringement at the time she would receive $\frac{3}{4}+2$ points. The penalties are cumulative, so a boat finishing last, say, having acknowledged two rule infringements receives $6+2+2$ points.

Under the existing points system there is no way of penalising a helmsman for a second infringement in a race. For example a boat which makes a blatant infringement on the start line and carries on will be disqualified, but anything she does after that first infringement will go unpenalised—she is already receiving the maximum penalty anyway. She could even cut corners on the course, miss marks out and so on to pull back to first place whenever her efforts at slowing the opposition took her to the back. And after being of enormous help to her teammates in this way she would only receive the same 10 points disqualification score as she would in sailing the rest of the race fairly after her initial infringement.

Presumably only the fear of being barred from clubs has prevented this happening so far.

Under the new system, you have three choices after being involved in an incident :

1. fly a red flag (meaning 'I am protesting')
2. fly a green flag ('I acknowledge I've broken a rule')
3. do nothing at all ('you can protest me if you like')

When a flag is flown it must be flown in reasonable time to be valid and the opposing helmsman must be made aware you are flying a flag. If you first fly a red flag but then decide within a reasonable time that you were in the wrong after all, you may take down your red flag and fly a green one, provided you make the opposing helmsman aware of the change. Once you've acknowledged an infringement with a green flag you can't decide to change and fly a red flag to protest.

So how does all this affect the racing? Well it means that an infringement acknowledged is equivalent in points to losing one place to an opponent. When you drop, say from 2nd to 3rd and an opponent climbs from 3rd to 2nd, you lose a point and he gains one, changing the difference between the teams by two points—the same as the penalty.

This may seem a very light penalty, and I originally suggested penalties of 3 and 6. But since then the 2 and 4 penalties have been used in five team competitions organised by Castaways and the only criticism seems to be that the lighter penalties take some of the needle out of the racing. Which is exactly what they were meant to do.

One possible abuse of the system is that when coming in to a mark on port tack, it would pay not to be put about by a starboard tack opponent, who would then hold you on past the mark, letting his teammate past. The loss to your team in this holding-on manoeuvre would be two places—4 points; the loss through accepting an infringement by ignoring all hails and holding the port tack would be 2, and you'd be ahead of both starboard black boats at the mark (a net gain when ignoring the right of way rule and conceding afterwards of 2 points).

Although this hasn't arisen in any of the two or three hundred matches so far sailed under the system, Castaways have slipped a clause into the sailing instructions to allow the fair sailing rule, 49, to be used in that case.

In the team meetings where this penalty system has been used there were fewer protests than under the usual retirement and disqualification system. The possible exception to that was the final weekend of the National Team Racing competition, when there were more protests than previous experience had indicated there would be. But generally in the competitions where the penalty system has been used helmsmen involved in a contentious incident who thought they were probably in the wrong promptly conceded their 2 penalty points, rather than risk taking the case to protest. Green flags were therefore fairly common, while the red ones that did appear didn't always result in a protest hearing, since the team had to be within 4 points of each other for the protest to affect the result. Under this system, winning depends on sailing skill. The incentive for the rule-pusher is taken away and everyone's happier—except of course the rule-pusher.

For anyone who wants to use the penalty system for their team races, here is a set of rules to govern its use. They were used in the finals of the 1973 RYA National Team Championships.

1 After any infringement of the rules, except an infringement mentioned in paragraphs 3 and 4 below, a yacht may acknowledge in reasonable time that she is to blame for the incident, accept two penalty points and continue racing, and show a green flag (see 7 below).

2 When an infringement is decided by protest the penalty points will be four.

3 A yacht disqualified for sailing unfairly (RYA rule 49), or causing serious damage (RYA rule 32) shall receive ten points plus any penalty points she accumulated during the race concerned.

4 A yacht disqualified for sailing the course incorrectly (including being over the line at the start and failing to return) shall receive eight points plus any penalty points accumulated during the race concerned.

5 A non-starter shall receive eight points.

6 If for any reason a team concedes a race to the opposing team without sailing, the team conceding the race will receive 24 points (3 non-starters—see 5 above). The team given a 'walk over' will receive 8 points in respect of that race. If the whole match (2 races) is conceded, the points received would be 48 and 16 respectively.

7 Penalty points are cumulative. If for example a yacht commits two infringements then both penalties will be added to her finishing score.

8 A green flag flown on a shroud signifies acknowledgement of blame and a racing rule infringement : a red flag signifies a protest. (Flags will be provided). A yacht which flies a flag must make every effort to draw the attention of other yachts involved in the incident to the flag. Flags must be flown within a reasonable time of the incident to which they refer. When a green flag is flown no protest may be brought concerning that incident except under RYA rules 49 and 32, in respect of which the protester should fly a red flag.

In time it is possible that the 720 degree turn alternative penalties may supersede this system.

I.Y.R.U. TEAM RACING RULES (1973)

Team racing shall be sailed under the yacht racing rules of the International Yacht Racing Union supplemented as follows:

SAILING RULES

1. A yacht may manoeuvre against a yacht sailing on another leg of the course only if she can do so while sailing a *proper course* relative to the leg on which she herself is sailing.

2. Except to protect her own or a team mate's finishing position, a yacht in one team which is completing the last leg of the course shall not manoeuvre against a yacht in another team which has no opponent astern of her.

3. When two *overlapping* yachts on the same *tack* are in the act of rounding or passing on the required side of a *mark* at which their *proper course* changes:

   (a)   If the *leeward yacht* is inside, she may, if she has *luffing* rights hold her course or *luff*. If she does not have *luffing* rights, she shall promptly assume her *proper course* to the next *mark* whether or not she has to *gybe*:

   (b)   If the *windward yacht* is inside, she shall promptly *luff* up to her *proper course* to the next *mark*, or if she cannot assume such *proper course* without *tacking* and does not choose to *tack*, she shall promptly *luff* up to *close-hauled*. This clause does not restrict a *leeward yacht's* right to *luff* under rule 38, Luffing after Starting.

SCORING

4. *Each Race*

(a) Yachts shall score three-quarters of a point for first place, two points for second place, three points for third place, and so on.

(b) A yacht which infringes any rule and retires with reasonable promptness shall score one point more than the number of yachts in the race, but in her retirement is tardy, or if she fails to retire and is subsequently disqualified, she shall score four points more than the number of yachts in the race.

(c) A yacht which infringes a rule shortly before or when *finishing* shall be considered to have retired with reasonable promptness if she notifies the race committee of her retirement as soon as is reasonably practicable.

(d) A yacht which does not *finish* for a reason other than an infringement shall score points equal to the number of starters in the race, except as provided in (e).

(e) After all the yachts of one team have *finished* or retired, the race committee may stop the race and allot to each yacht of the other team which is still *racing* and under way the points she would have received had she *finished*.

5. *The Series*

(a) When only two teams are competing, the team winning the greater number of races sailed shall be the winner of the series.

(b) When three or more teams are competing in a series consisting of races each of which is between two teams, the team winning the greatest number of races shall be the winner.

(c) When three or more teams are all competing in each race the team with the lowest total point score in all races sailed shall be the winner.

6. *Breaking Ties*

When two or more teams are tied because each has won the same number of races, if practicable, the tie should be resolved by a sail off.

If there is a tie when more than two teams are competing, the team which has beaten the other tied team or teams in the most races shall be the winner. Failing this, the team with the lowest point score in all races sailed shall be the winner. When teams tie with only two teams competing and a sail off is impracticable, the tie shall be broken in favour of the winner of the last race.

ADDENDUM
RULES RECOMMENDED TO APPLY WHEN THE HOME TEAM FURNISHES ALL RACING YACHTS

A. *Assignment of Yachts.* The home team shall furnish the visiting team with a list of the yachts to be used and of the sail numbers assigned to each yacht for the match. The home team shall divide these yachts into as many equal groups as there are competing teams and these groups shall be drawn for by lot for the first race. Skipper assignment to the yachts shall then be made as each team decides for itself, except that a skipper shall not at any time sail his own yacht. The groups of yachts shall be exchanged between races so that, as far as possible, each group will be sailed in turn by each team. In a two team match after an even number of races, if either team requests that the yachts be regrouped, the home team shall re-divide them into new groups which shall be drawn for by lot; except that for the final odd race of a two team match, the visiting team may select the group it wishes to sail.

B. *Assignment of Sails.* If sails as well as yachts are furnished by the home team, the sails used by each yacht in the first race shall be used by her throughout the series and the substitution of a spare or extra sail shall not be permitted unless because of damage or for some other valid reason, a change is approved by the Jury or Judges after notification to both teams.

C. *Group Identification.* One group shall carry no marking. The second group shall carry dark coloured strips or pennants, and additional groups shall carry light or differently coloured strips or pennants. Strips or pennants should usually be furnished by the home team and should be attached to the same conspicuous place on each boat of a group, such as the after end of the main boom or permanent backstay.

D. *Breakdowns.* When a breakdown results in substantial loss, the Jury or Judges shall decide whether or not it was the fault of the crew. In general, a breakdown caused by defective equipment, or the result of a foul by an opponent shall not be deemed the fault of the crew, and a breakdown caused by careless handling or capsizing shall be. In case of doubt, the doubt shall be resolved in favour of the crew.

E. If the Jury or Judges decide that the breakdown was not the fault of the crew and that a reasonably competent crew could not have remedied the defect in time to prevent substantial loss, they shall cancel the race, or order it to be resailed, or award the breakdown yacht the number of points she would have received had she finished in the same position in the race she held when she broke down. In case of doubt as to her position when she broke down, the doubt shall be resolved against her.

F. *Spares.* The home team shall be prepared to furnish one or more extra yachts and sails to replace any which, in the opinion of the Jury or Judges, are unfit for use in the remaining races.